Life. Land. Legacy.

Home to Us

SIX STORIES *of* SAVING *the* LAND

Photographed by Nancy Rhoda
Written by Varina Willse

THE LAND TRUST FOR TENNESSEE

HOME TO US: SIX STORIES OF SAVING THE LAND

Photographed by Nancy Rhoda
Written by Varina Willse

This is a nonfiction book about six families and their land in Tennessee. It was photographed, written, edited and designed over an extended period of time prior to August 2012, when it was printed and bound in Nashville under the sponsorship of The Land Trust for Tennessee, a state-wide, private, 501(c)(3) non-profit organization whose mission is to preserve the unique character of Tennessee's natural and historic landscapes and sites for future generations.

Library of Congress Control Number: 2012942141

International Standard Book Number (ISBN): 978-0-615-65722-6

Produced and Manufactured in Nashville, Tennessee, USA
Graphic Design by Bill Kersey, KerseyGraphics
Printing by Lithographics, LLC
Binding by BINDTECH, Inc.

First Edition, First Printing: August 2012

Contents

Introduction

When I was a child growing up in Middle Tennessee half a century ago, I felt most at home and most myself when I was in the great outdoors— on lakes and rivers, in rolling meadows and dense green woods. Whether I was building fires at Camp Nakanawa on the Cumberland Plateau or pressing leaves in high-school biology lab, it was the wondrous depth and beauty of nature that claimed my attention.

I first lived in a tiny white house in the middle of a field (transformed now into a suburban Nashville neighborhood). Our next home was on the edge of the Warner Parks, and I practically lived in the woods there, climbing maples and building hideaways with my friends. Summers we spent at my grandmother's in Monteagle, and family vacations took us to many of the state's natural parks. My literal grounding as a young person came from being as close to the earth as I could get—hiking, camping, swimming.

Those early experiences resurfaced as I was finishing my years of formal education and choosing a career. As a young lawyer, I couldn't help but focus on environmental concerns. In the fields of legislation and public policy, my energy seemed to flow into programs aimed at preserving the natural beauty of Tennessee.

I even married a lawyer—with a passion for the environment. My husband, Will Martin, was deeply engaged in land conservation issues long before we married. From the start, including our honeymoon, we spent our vacations backpacking and mountain-climbing in remote places—landscapes of true solitude—and those experiences were life-shaping. We instinctively knew that such vistas can't protect themselves; they need the stewardship of a caring society.

Wanting to apply these values to our professional lives, Will and I volunteered our services in the early 1990s to Nashville's new mayor, Phil

Bredesen. He put us to work searching for tracts of land in Davidson County that might be purchased and "banked" to become parks and greenways over the next century. The endeavor involved a bit of discreet trespassing into some remote corners of the county, but eventually resulted in the addition of two new open spaces—Shelby Bottoms and Beaman Park—to the park system of Metropolitan Nashville.

That was my first experience of what it really means to "save the land," and it was an intensely gratifying one. Working with others, in and out of government, to protect land for the future benefit of the public became my ideal vision of service, and my professional calling. This sense of purpose took me to Washington, D.C., where I gained a broader view of the impact of industrial practices on our national lands. As a result, two recurring insights became firm convictions for me. One was the crucial importance of allowing some open spaces to remain as they are—in agriculture, forests, watersheds, parks. The other was that the most successful decisions of this nature are the ones that originate at the local level.

Eventually, I would come to believe that the most effective and lasting way to conserve land is through carefully tailored legal agreements between landowners committed to preservation and nonprofit organizations dedicated to protecting natural resources and historic sites. But when Will and I returned to Nashville in 1998, that particular method had not yet crystallized for me. I only knew that Tennessee was where I wanted to be, and where I wanted to put my experiences to the test.

When I was a young lawyer, I had a mentor over whose shoulder hung an arresting quotation from T. S. Eliot. It read, "We shall not cease from exploration, and the end of all our exploring will be to arrive where we started and know the place for the first time." I copied it, even carried it for a time in my wallet, without really knowing why—until a December evening in 1998, when I finally discovered what it meant. Sitting in Mayor Phil Bredesen's living room that evening, I realized that I had come to the end of my exploring.

The mayor and his wife, Andrea Conte, had invited a few friends and associates in for an evening of talk. It was a pleasant social occasion, but more: These were people whose land-preservation values were similar to his. In his low-key manner, Bredesen brought us around to the subject he was intent on discussing: land trusts, a time-honored strategy of preservation in other parts of the country, including his native Northeast, and abroad. It was a concept that I knew of, but only vaguely.

The mayor explained that for well over a century, designated trustees have safeguarded hallowed ground by creating a legal mechanism to provide for its perpetual stewardship. In Wyoming's Grand Tetons, he had observed first-hand the benefits of protective easements adjacent to that mountain range. Here at home, he also knew that former Tennessee Governor Lamar Alexander had drawn upon the land trust principle to protect some Smoky Mountain foothills near his hometown of Maryville. The most effective way to preserve our major landmarks for future generations, Bredesen concluded, was not by political means but through partnerships between public and private interests.

Bredesen wanted to embrace that concept, with a broader application. It was still about protecting a historic village here, an old forest there, a spectacular waterfall or a century-old family farm somewhere else—but collectively, these treasured assets would become the framework for safeguarding the entire state's historical and geographical identity. As I listened, The Land Trust for Tennessee came to life for me, right then and there. I had arrived where I started, and I knew the place for the first time.

The following year, The Land Trust was formally chartered as a private, nonprofit organization. At the first board meeting, we put our mission into words: "To preserve the unique character of Tennessee's natural and historic landscapes and sites for future generations." We grabbed a catchy phone number—244-LAND—and set about getting an official address in the historic Cummins Station building in Nashville. Our only option at the time was a closet-sized room, but by coincidence or by providence, we met members of the Corby family, whose technology business was housed there. When they discovered what we were trying to do, they took us in, generously providing us both a bigger workspace and a website.

Now, thirteen years later, The Land Trust has succeeded beyond the most ambitious dreams of its founder, directors, volunteers and extraordinary staff. In concert with over two hundred property owners, we have developed and applied a legal framework—the conservation easement—for the protection of almost 75,000 Tennessee acres, assuring that these landscapes, whether privately or publicly owned, will never lose their physical and functional identity. In some instances, The Land Trust is also buying tracts of land for later transfer to local government park systems or state agencies.

Collectively, these "saves" guarantee that an expanding portion of our state's geographic and historic treasures, some of which are older than the state itself, will still look the same centuries from now. The vast majority of these sites are privately owned, and thus remain on the property-tax rolls. But the proprietors and all others who may come to own them in the future can be confident that nothing will ever alter the land's identity. What it has been, it will be. Forever. For most of the owners, this is the greatest legacy they can pass on to their descendants and their community.

Many of the parcels preserved by The Land Trust are profoundly natural and authentic—and so are the people who own and protect them. These are people with a deep sense of family roots and history, but who also have, above all else, a desire to do something lasting. Each family and each parcel is its own compelling story. Which is why, almost from the beginning, we have wanted to put some of these personal accounts into words and pictures, so we could share them more broadly. Now at last we have done that, and the result is here in your hands.

Home to Us: Six Stories of Saving the Land focuses on a small number of Middle Tennessee families, their histories, and their ultimate decisions, arrived at individually and expressed in a variety of ways, to make the land their chosen legacy. We look upon these six in-depth portraits as representative examples of all our partners in this endeavor. You will find a complete list of them in The Land Trust Honor Roll in the back of the book.

Our creative team for the development of this book begins with Nancy Rhoda, a dear friend and The Land Trust's principal photographer for more than a decade. Nancy took all the pictures in this volume, with the exception of the historic ones. The book's author, Varina Willse, grew up on her family's farm in Robertson County (the sixth generation of Buntins to live there). When she and I first talked about the project nearly four years ago, she was immediately drawn to the personal stories of these Tennesseans so devoted to saving their land. She was a natural choice to visit with the families and weave their stories for us.

These two, working closely with veteran Nashville editor John Egerton, graphic designer Bill Kersey and production coordinator Ellen Bradbury at Lithographics, our chosen printer, have given us a book that is both a labor of love and a true work of art. It is a rich tapestry of Tennessee stories, woven in a seamless blend of words and images.

The meaning and relevance of these stories extend beyond our state to the entire South and Nation, exploring as they do the timeless universal connection between people and place, between the natural world and the way we live in it. To read them is to recognize the vital importance of maintaining these connections.

As with most people the world over, Tennesseans care deeply about their land, whether it literally belongs to them or is symbolically theirs—their rivers and parks, forests, meadows, mountain ranges. Their homeland is an extension of themselves, and they want it to retain its appearance and character for all time. In that, The Land Trust is their willing and able partner.

Jeanie Nelson
President

The Crunk Family

Hard Work & Clean Livin'

When a stranger to the farming community of Bethesda in rural Williamson County first meets Mrs. Elizabeth Crunk, he can't help but be struck by her. She is elderly, in a chronological sense, but vigorously attractive, with blue-gray eyes blazing out of a weather-worn face. A thick mat of white hair bulges from beneath her ball cap, which has a cow emblazoned on the front, and her pearled earrings offset the brogans she's wearing.

The stranger—a visitor from the Netherlands just picking up on Southern lingo—makes bold to ask her, in a friendly sort of way, "Are you a Tennessee hillbilly?"

Mrs. Crunk is certainly a Tennessean. But of the two farms where she has spent the past nine-plus decades of her life, only one is hilly. The other is flat. And so, hand on hip, she gives the man a mischievous smile and decides to mess with him a bit, while also setting the record straight. It's a combination of sass and straight-shooting she mastered long ago—at least as early as age fifteen, when she, Elizabeth, made her teacher, "Miz Oliver," cry because she refused to take her feet out of a bucket of cold water in the home ec room. It was frostbite weather, and, as usual, Elizabeth had ridden her horse to school. Along the way her feet froze. She was thawing them according to her daddy's advice, and no amount of cajoling or crying by the teacher was going to get her to do otherwise. That headstrong girl is now the woman confronting the question, "Are you a Tennessee hillbilly?"

"Well, yes. I really am," she says, "But I'm a Tennessee *Clodhoppa* Hillbilly."

Naturally, the man has a second question: "What's a Clodhoppa?"

The word, of course, is *clodhopper*, which the man wouldn't have recognized anyway, but Mrs. Crunk's voice has a circular, saw-like quality to it, as if her top jaw holds tight and her bottom jaw does the grinding, a good Southern grinding, so that the words that come out are sometimes chewed off or cut on the bias and therefore hard to understand. Compound that with the fact that Mrs. Crunk gains momentum with each word in a story when the story is a good one, which it almost always is, and so the particulars occasionally get lost. The gist, however, never does.

"Well, I was born in flatland on the same road that I live on now," she explains, her hands rising naturally to participate in the telling. "When it got dry and hot in the summatime, if you had ground that was worked up and plowed, well, you've got big clods that you got to hop over until you get 'em beat up. Then, when I married and moved two miles up the road in the hills, I got the hills plus the clodhoppa, so I'm a Tennessee Clodhoppa Hillbilly."

Elizabeth McCord, age seventeen, alongside her high school sweetheart and future husband Johnny Crunk.

These last three words she delivers slowly, then cuts her eyes and holds. Those eyes have a twinkle, like sunlight bobbing along a fresh spring. The lines around them have deepened, both from age and from a life spent farming, both from laughing and from gritting through things painful.

Elizabeth McCord was born on January 16, 1919 on Cedar Lane Farm, where she was raised by her parents and her grandmother. In 1940, she married a boy from school, John Henry Crunk Jr., known as Johnny, and the two of them bought a second farm a couple of miles up the road that they called Hill View Farm. As soon as Johnny was discharged from the Army in 1946, the two returned to Hill View and built first a home and then a Grade A dairy. All of those people—Elizabeth's grandmother, her parents, and her husband—have since passed on, some earlier than is right, some later than averages would have predicted. Mrs. Crunk will be in the latter camp, but at 91, she is hardly taking it easy.

Nailed to the door of her tool shed is a sign:

> *Life should NOT be a journey to the grave with the intention of arriving safely in an attractive and well preserved body, but rather to skid in sideways…body thoroughly used up, totally worn out and screaming, 'WOO HOO, what a ride!'*

Married sixty years, Annie Lou and Walker McCord stand behind their two daughters, Dorothy and Elizabeth, and their son-in-law, Johnny.

In a number of ways, Mrs. Crunk's body isn't well preserved. "I do it in twos, you see," she says lightheartedly, referring to the breaking of her bones. When she and Johnny ran the dairy, a bull she had "raised as a pet" charged her and broke both of her arms (plus a bone in her back). Decades later, at 86, she broke her leg but did well with it until she fell in 2009 and broke the other leg, also pulling the hip-ball out of socket. She lives alone so when she fell, she had to drag herself across the kitchen floor to the hallway, knock the phone off its hook, then toss a coat over the grate where she would lie waiting for the ambulance to come. "I called 911 and I didn't have to call 'em but one time cause I was yellin'! And I've laughed about that," she says, laughing about it again. "Of all the bills that you get and how much everything is, I said 'Well, the only cheap thing I got was 911. That didn't cost but 94 cents.'" She jokes about it, but the pain she experienced was so intense that it knocked her heart out of rhythm.

Add to the two broken arms, two broken legs, dizzy heart and frostbitten feet, not only poor hearing in both ears but a good deal of lost teeth. This last condition in particular might have proven disheartening for someone

Mrs. Crunk admits that using a walker "flusterates" her, but she is not about to let it stop her from doing the yard work she so loves.

who always ate an apple first thing in the morning, usually around 3:30 a.m., but Mrs. Crunk just eats applesauce now and keeps on. As a result of this brand of perseverance and a recipe of "hard work and clean livin'" she learned from her mother, Mrs. Crunk's body, broken bones and all, is less "thoroughly used up and totally worn out" than it is unbelievably strong and able. That, or her tolerance for pain is off the charts, or a bit of both.

Mrs. Crunk first heard this phrase "hard work and clean livin'" in her mother's answer to the question of how she had managed to live to be 100 years old. It has been Mrs. Crunk's answer to life as well. She is a proponent of natural foods—celery to improve circulation, fermented soybeans to take care of the heart. Her only medications are home remedies— "black ointment" for infections and "silver" to ward off colds. She warns against the dangers of chemicals and the addictive quality of painkillers.

More fundamentally, though, she warns against the dangers of giving up: "If you just say, I'm just going to retire and sit down and rock, well, you've soon rocked out."

Which is why Mrs. Crunk insists on getting out in her yard even if she has to use a walker to do it. In her sun hat and long sleeves and Earth shoes, she takes on the dandelions and the moles foolish enough to choose her soil as home. She totes buckets back and forth to the shed and busies herself with the flowerbeds before making her way down to the barn. There she maneuvers along the fence until she reaches the riding mower. Mrs. Crunk runs the risk of it quitting on her and leaving her stranded in the middle of the field

without her walker, which it has done, but she isn't daunted. She hops on, taking the turns deftly, taking matters into her own hands: a woman clearly not ready to end this ride.

I Got You

Elizabeth Crunk's earliest memories take her back to rides with her grandmother, though the two of them were in a horse-and-buggy not on a John Deere. Elizabeth remembers leaving for town early, when the sky hadn't

yet started its wakeful stretching. She can't recall why they were making the trip into town, but she remembers the tollgates on the road, and she remembers that Granny tied her in, using the buggy rug as a makeshift seatbelt.

Mrs. Crunk has a string of stories from those days that she loves to tell, many of which center around this pivotal figure in her life, "the one that I stayed under her coattails." In these stories, Granny is always associated with Baptist Rest, the original name for the old homestead that her father, Elizabeth's great-grandfather, had bought in the late 1800s.

"I remember that house so well," Mrs. Crunk says, eyes twinkling. "It had seventeen rooms, a porch downstairs and upstairs, too, in the front. It had a catwalk—a catwalk or dog trot, whichever you wanna call it—between the house and the brick kitchen. And when you went in the front hall, all this winding steps, stairway, you know. Oh, we would scoot down those banisters when my cousins would come. I remember that." Mrs. Crunk still has one of the original bricks from the kitchen, along with an oil lamp and a few pieces of her grandmother's china, but not much else—including almost no family photographs—as a result of a house fire that consumed it in the early 1920s.

The story of the fire has little nostalgia to it now, having been repeated so many times. It is, instead, her go-to tale, one of the old favorites right down to the bit about the roasted hams. But even more, this story is emblematic of the kind of person Mrs. Crunk is, the kind of person she has always been: the chin-up, move-on kind, impervious to self-pity.

"It was the last day of March but it was awfully windy like some of the winds we've had this year," Mrs. Crunk tells, settling into the familiar lines. "Granny got up to put a stick of wood on the fireplace and of course it had shingles on top, you know, like people are doing now again. That's how they think it happened. They rang the dinner bell outside but by the time people got there, it was so much fire with that big a place, you see, couldn't nobody do nothin'. My mother was pregnant at the time. We were going up the lane, walking along and mother was just a-cryin', and she said I said, 'Well mother, what's the matter?' And she said, 'Well, honey, you won't have any Easter shoes.' She said, 'Don't you know your little shoes were in that chest drawer. You won't have any Easter shoes and you won't have any new little new dress or nothin'.' Said, 'We won't have anything; it's all burnin' up.'"

Mrs. Crunk knows this story less from her own memory than from her mother's, but she interweaves the dialogue as naturally as a needle pulls thread. "Mother said I said, 'Well my goodness, mother. That don't make no difference. I got you.' And she would tell that." Mrs. Crunk pauses before proudly repeating her last line, "Well, that don't make no difference, I got you."

Mrs. Crunk's grandmother, Laura Walker McCord, who operated the Century Farm.

But she isn't finished. "So the hams were all up in there. Back then you didn't leave your hams in the smokehouse… cause people were bad about stealin' em. And course they cooked. All the ashes blowed away from the fire; it was so windy that day. And here lay these big hams. So we ate em!" she says with a cackle. "I remember eatin' the meat."

No Easter shoes and no house, but the McCords did have each other and some cooked ham and a good story. It's a story that speaks to the resilience of both Elizabeth and her grandmother. "She kept on. She didn't let it get her down," Mrs. Crunk says. Granny didn't let it get her down when her husband passed away, leaving her with a young son and daughter, and she didn't let it get her down when her house burned. "She was a strong woman, a hard-working woman," Mrs. Crunk continues. "She had rheumatism in the knees so bad she could hardly walk.

But she'd pull her shoes off and go in the garden and get peas and beans when it was too wet to be in there."

Mrs. Crunk does recognize that this sounds familiar. "And so, I am a whole lot of my grandmother."

My Way

Unlike her grandmother, Elizabeth did not have young children when her husband passed away, but much like her grandmother, she did have a farm to run. And in Mrs. Crunk's case, a whole lot of cows to care for. "When Johnny died we was milkin' 45 Jerseys…And I had another 45 heifers across the road and 20 babies in the pen."

Elizabeth's father, who was not a dairyman but a carpenter and bricklayer, was not alone in his concern that perhaps his daughter couldn't handle the dairy farm by herself. As Elizabeth tells it, he would come over every morning and sit outside the barn where she did the milking, whittle on a stick, and give unsolicited advice.

"Get rid of them cows," he would tell her. "They're killin' you."

"Milkin's not hurting me," she would answer, but the next morning it would be the same thing. "He'd be sitting out there whittlin' away, and I'd have to be running to feed a calf."

"Well, you're killin' yourself," he would tell her.

"So the next morning I thought, well I ain't gonna listen to that. So I get goin', get the milkers goin', and I go out and I said, 'Daddy, I gotta talk to you.'"

"Well you gotta get rid of these cows."

"I said, 'Now listen, that's what I'm gonna talk about. I'm not-a-gonna get rid of the cows til September. I'm gonna run this place. I don't care what anybody says. MY WAY. If Dick, Tom and Harry tells me I'm turning up a ditch the wrong way, that's fine. Because, I'm the one that's gonna have to be payin' the taxes. And I'm gonna run it MY WAY.'"

It was at this moment that her daddy exclaimed, "Well, that's what I've been waitin' to hear!" Walker McCord knew, right then and there, that

his daughter could handle both herself and the land just fine. He needn't come whittling and meddling outside the barn door at 4 a.m. any longer.

Mrs. Crunk learned her "way" in part from her father, a man who built several houses and barns in the community, notoriously pulling out any nail that was even slightly bent in order to replace it with a straight one.

Iconic and enduring, the red barn on Highway 431 was built by Mrs. Crunk's father over eighty years ago, before there was electricity.

He was the one to teach her never to climb over a fence but always to use the gate. And the one who indirectly made her seek out the services of The Land Trust.

"I heard my Daddy say one day, 'I don't want this place cut up in little squares.' But I didn't know how I was going to get that," she says. She spent years searching for ways to fulfill her father's desire, and though she had read about land trusts in other states, Tennessee had yet to enact its own. According to her niece Bettye Cason, Mrs. Crunk spent "at least ten years looking for something, some way to preserve, some way to keep this all in the family. Some way that she could pass it on."

The two now like to boast that their conservation easement was the quickest The Land Trust had ever completed, with the paperwork wrapped up in under seven months. "She knew exactly what she wanted," Bettye says. "A lot of people you've got to walk them through…but she knew exactly what she wanted done and how she wanted it done."

Laughing, Mrs. Crunk does admit that she had to send the papers back to the lawyer twice because the wording wasn't exactly as she wanted it. He had understood that someone could cut timber off the land for firewood, but Mrs. Crunk was quick to correct him. "Only thing you can cut for fire-wood is something that has blown down or is dead. There's a big difference right there," she rightfully insists.

The details now done, Mrs. Crunk stresses that the conservation easement means one thing to her: security. And Bettye adds, "It's not only security for her. It's security for me. It's security even for my kids and grandkids. And on down the line."

As with running the farm, Mrs. Crunk figured out how to save it. Her way. "It's not for everybody," Mrs. Crunk suggests. "But a lot more people need to do it."

All Natural

Elizabeth has always done things her way, even when her way was little known or understood. In fact, there wasn't even a word for Mrs. Crunk's approach to farming when she started it, though now it would be called "eco-friendly."

"I have headwaters," she explains. "See, two springs are on this place: that's called headwaters, and it goes to the Duck River. If you don't keep the headwaters clean, why the river's not gonna be clean." Mrs. Crunk was cognizant of this fact long ago, when she realized what it would take to maintain a farm with hills. Unlike the Cedar Lane Farm, this farm, the one she and Johnny bought in 1943 and aptly called Hill View Farm, appears to have large waves cresting beneath the ground. The effect is picturesque for a visitor but challenging for a farmer.

"This farm, being a hill farm, was really washin' away," Mrs. Crunk explains. "My husband worked for a tobacco company, and he had a ton-and-a-half truck, so during tobacco season, he hauled in all the tobacco stalks he could haul." The Crunks then used those stalks to create a hill-side terrace in order to redirect the water. They also transferred truckloads of hay to fill in the gullies and ditches. "This is the way you've got to farm a hill," Mrs. Crunk says. "Because if you put commercial fertilizer on it, and it comes a rainin', it's going to wind up in the creek or river. So we just started doin' that. And so, that's just what we always done."

Mrs. Crunk didn't rely on common sense alone; she was proactive in learning how to farm her land naturally. As soon as Johnny returned home from the Army, she started subscribing to *Organic Gardening* and *Rodale's* and began reading Ruth Stout's books. "I tried to keep all toxins out of the pastures and weeds and everything," she says. "I didn't wanna kill the earthworms. There are seven different things in the soil that you don't even know about that are workin' to keep the soil like it should be."

Mrs. Crunk knew, for instance, that the filler in the groundfeed she gave her cows was made from the byproduct of cornstarch, which happens to be a natural herbicide. "So when the cows eat that feed and it come out in manure, you didn't have a lot of weeds comin' up," she explains.

Ten or so years ago, when Mrs. Crunk was working at the Garden Center at Kmart, she had a customer ask her what weed killer she used. Kmart didn't carry the product, so Mrs. Crunk stopped at three different places after she got off work to find it for the man. Every clerk she asked either had no idea what she was talking about or thought she had no idea what

Mrs. Crunk continues to haul hay for filling in ditches, backbreaking work she insists on doing in order to prevent erosion.

The bush hogging done and the shadows lengthening, Mrs. Crunk can now retire her work gloves for the day.

she was talking about or both. In true Mrs. Crunk fashion, she resolved to "fix all that." So when she found what she was looking for, an organic herbicide called Concern, she bought four bags of it. She took each bag, one by one, back to those stores and plopped it down on the counter for the managers to see.

"When I got to Tractor Supply," she tells, "the guy said, 'Well Mrs. Crunk, I didn't know what you were talkin' about.' I said, 'I know you didn't and that's the reason I'm showin' you that I'm not a crazy old woman.'

Because, you know, women don't know much." Here she pauses, leaving a hole for you to plant your laugh.

Ever since Johnny's death, there have been people along the way who have thought, like her father initially did, that she wouldn't be able to keep up certain aspects of the farming life. As Bettye puts it, "The neighbors, when my uncle died, thought, well, she's a woman, she can't do nothin'. I think over the years the neighbors have realized she's smarter than they thought she was." She gives an example to prove her point. "There used to be a ditch right here between these two hills. It was over my head. You could've drove a tractor-trailer down through it and not seen the tractor-trailer. And you can drive a tractor across it now and bush hog." Who filled it in? Mrs. Crunk. And who has been the one to bush hog it? She has.

Bush Hoggin'

It was back in 1952 when Elizabeth Crunk first got on a tractor. She and Johnny recognized that machinery was slowly taking the place of mules and horses for farming labor and so they got one. "That's the awfullest racket I ever heard!" Johnny proclaimed upon hearing it started, so Elizabeth said, "Well, let me try it." He agreed but on certain conditions: she was not to exceed the boundaries he laid out with his plow, boundaries that would keep her off the steep inclines of their sloped property.

"He never did bush hog another day," Mrs. Crunk reports. "That was 1952. And he died suddenly with a heart attack in 1975." She says these words matter of factly, with the fact of the matter being that she was the one to do the bush hogging those twenty-three years they were still married.

Johnny and Elizabeth returned home from the Army in 1946.

Elizabeth doesn't talk much about their courtship or their wedding. She doesn't talk much about Johnny's personality or his passing, other than to say that several members of Johnny's family died of heart attacks, he and his mother both at age 57, he and his brother both on February 11. She starts to tell of Johnny having a premonition of his own death, but she interrupts herself to point at a squirrel and never finishes.

One story she does like to tell is about the time she sneaked on the troop train, subtly falling into march behind her husband in order to ride with him from Florida to Washington. The conductor stumbled upon her in the middle of the night, the only woman in a train full of soldiers, and thought she was a "pick up." It took several kicks to Johnny's leg before he woke up enough to validate that she was indeed his wife. "And I rode into Washington, D.C. on that train," she tells triumphantly. "Now that's a tale but that's the truth!"

Mrs. Crunk affirms that she and Johnny had something special and that knowing how to ride the tractor helped her move forward after his death. "If I hadn't of known how to do that," she says of bush hogging, "I'd have been a lost sheep." It's a metaphor she understands fully since Mrs. Crunk has raised and looked after sheep as well as cattle. That tractor, and more largely her knowing how to maintain the farm, allowed Mrs. Crunk to disprove those people who dismissed her as a woman who therefore "can't do nothin'." In keeping with her own analogy, this farming know-how has been Elizabeth Crunk's shepherd and her savior.

Now, it has been half-a-century and then some that Mrs. Crunk has been bush hogging the 151 acres that comprise Hill View Farm. She has been known to stop the tractor mid-pasture, get off, and pull a weed most people wouldn't notice walking. She is that conscientious, that tuned in. And she is that dedicated. For decades after Johnny's death, Mrs. Crunk would go to work all day—as a postal worker, as the manager of the Goose Creek Inn, as a salesperson at the Garden Center—come home and get to the business of bush hogging. She would take care of ill relatives or cook Thanksgiving dinner, then get back out there and bush hog. As late as 10:00 at night, there would be the faded silhouette of Mrs. Crunk on her tractor, the steady sound of it humming on the darkening air.

T and Sug

It is for this reason, this promise of self-sufficiency and empowerment, that Mrs. Crunk wants to teach Jaida, her great, great, great, great niece, the ways of farming life, too—much in the way that her Granny had taught her. "I sat on the rock and helped Granny like Jaida helps me now," Mrs. Crunk says, remembering when she was a little girl how the two of them would "shell peas and beans and churn and fix chickens," lowering the food into the well where it would keep overnight. So many generations later, Mrs. Crunk, or "T" as Jaida calls her, is able to pass along that same kind of wisdom and love.

Mrs. Crunk has ample opportunity because she watches four-year-old Jaida four or five days a week—no job for the weary. There is no watching TV to speak of, nor is there much resting. This afternoon, for instance, they plan to take one of the gourds the two of them planted last year and turn it into a birdhouse. Jaida, who arrives at T's in flip flops with her hair down, has in no time pulled it back with a Co-op cap and is toting tools in her gloved hands.

"We're going to put it right up here, Sug," Mrs. Crunk says to Jaida, using the abbreviated form of the affectionate term, Sugar. She holds the gourd down where Jaida can see and explains how they will go about their work. "We can make a hole, see here, and put a string through it. We may not can put that back on. But, we gonna blow a hole right here for the little bird's nest."

The broken gourd they plan to revive could easily have been tossed aside. But looking around Mrs. Crunk's yard, numerous items others might have deemed useless have been put to work: rusted mattress springs turned into a trellis, old pitchers transformed into planters, empty bottles added to an African bottle tree to scare away evil spirits. It's a place where things aren't just saved, they are *used*, continuing to function, continuing to live.

Mrs. Crunk and her niece Jaida have just finished planting salvia, a flower that holds special memories for Mrs. Crunk of her mother.

Resting the gourd on the old springs in the yard, T and Sug hold the neck and body together, feeling the two parts slide back into place like reversing time. "There, there it goes," T exclaims, with mounting enthusiasm. "Look. We can tape that back on. Look at it, Sug! We can fix it good." T goes to retrieve a brace and bit, not thinking twice about making the trip to the basement herself. Returning with a drill and now with the help of Jaida's grandmother, the three women form a huddle, the taped gourd at their center.

"Hold your hand up here, Sug," T says to Jaida, tapping at the side of the gourd. And the two sets of hands, so many generations apart, come together bracing against the power of the drill. Jaida strains as her determination slips. "I can't hold this for long," she says.

"Yes, Sug, you can," T tells her. "You're doing alright, honey."

And before they know it, they have successfully made a new birdhouse to hang from one of T's trees. Add gathering cowpies to cover the exposed roots of trees in the front yard, more planting in the garden, and the occasional joy ride on the riding mower, and you have a typical day for T and Sug. Mrs. Crunk has worried that Jaida isn't ready for school, that she isn't at the reading level she should be, but the teacher assures her that what Jaida is learning there—about how to identify birds and how eggshells help in composting—is far more important. The rest will come; the rest is easy.

Sit Awhile

The rest, however, in its most literal sense, has not come easy for Mrs. Crunk. She is a worker by nature, a "hustler" as her farm manager says, a woman who stops for nothing but another task that needs doing.

Not too long ago, Mrs. Crunk was six months shy of being eligible for retirement from the post office. She had begun a mail route at 65 and spent the next fourteen years as a postal worker, while also keeping up the farm and looking after her aging mother. She went into her room one morning, and her mother told her flatly that she didn't want her to work anymore. "I said, 'Mother. Who's gonna open the PO this morning? Who's gonna work

The last ritual of the day, Jaida retrieves "T's" mail for her, and the two share a hug and a kiss goodbye.

those PO boxes? Who's gonna sell stamps? Who's gonna take care of the customers?'"

Mrs. Crunk recalls her mother saying, "'That's right. You do have to do that. You go and you do that but you call Nashville and tell them you're quittin' and you come home.' And that's what I done," Mrs. Crunk affirms. Half-a-year before qualifying for retirement, she quit, but only because she had other, more important work to do. "I don't have any regrets. Because she lived until the next July and we had a lot of good days. I got to lift her outta bed and now I laugh about that because she was so scared that I was gonna drop her. I said, 'Now mother I'm not gonna drop you. I'm gonna lift you and put you in that wheelchair just as easy.' And I did. And it wadn't no trouble."

Mrs. Crunk didn't leave her mother from November until July, when her life of hard work and clean livin' came to its peaceful end. "She lived to be 102, 6 months and 21 days," Mrs. Crunk proudly tells.

Mrs. Crunk believes that she, like her mother, has been given extra health and strength. Talking to a neighbor recently, she announced that if she lived eighteen years longer than her mother, then she would live to be 120. The neighbor apparently gave her an incredulous grunt, because Mrs. Crunk answered, "Well, who knows! Sarah in the Bible lived to be 120. And that's the only woman in the Bible that they tell her age!"

For now though, Mrs. Crunk does something she never used to do, something she has earned. Rather than ride the tractor, or head off to work or come home from work, or go visit her mother, or pull weeds, or plant potatoes, or tend to her cows, Mrs. Crunk sits down.

She has a particular seat, one fashioned from an old hay rake that she found in a ditch. She has it positioned in her yard so that looking out, she can see past a number of crests to the Duck River ridge. It is the place

where the headwaters on her property flow, the river she has personally helped keep clean. From her vantage point, she can also see the low-lying town of Columbia.

"I see the lights at night," she says. "See how relaxin' it is." And, for a time, for perhaps the first time, she does let herself rest and breathe in her clean farm air.

A master of interior design and an impeccable host, Lannie Neal awaits dinner guests at his home outside Leiper's Fork.

The Neal Family

Stark Contrast

Lannie Neal begins his day with five games of solitaire. If he wins a majority, it will be a great day. If he loses a majority, it won't; simple as that. Too fun-loving to be a fatalist, Lannie admits that this fortune-telling habit of his is strange, maybe even "a little crazy," but he can't help himself. He's so taken with the accuracy of it that he keeps a record of his wins and losses in a journal.

Should that journal extend back thirteen years, it would likely reveal a five-game winning streak on the day he first bought land in Maury County. Lannie thought he was buying the property to serve as hunting land for his sons. He wasn't interested in keeping any for himself because he was leaving town, leaving the country for that matter, to move to a chateau in France.

Just prior to departing for Paris to confirm the sale, however, he discovered an unfortunate glitch that must have been in the cards. "They weren't going to sell the chateau to anybody that lived outside of this little nucleus of that part of France," Lannie says with an unaffected shrug. "So I said, well, forget it." With that, he came back to Tennessee and informed his sons, Andrew and Matthew, that their hunting camp was off; he would be calling zip code 38401 home.

At the time, which was 1998, the property had only half of a barn and an incredibly steep hill, along with acre after acre of native forest. Choosing the hilltop as his building site, Lannie solicited Matthew's help to engineer the complicated water system needed to defy gravity. "It wasn't the Alaskan pipeline but for us it was a hell of a project," Matthew says, looking back on it. But neither father nor son was deterred.

Passionate about all things French, Lannie shares the history of his home's Versailles-inspired architectural elements.

Lannie had recently discovered a log house being dismantled in Lincoln County, so he bought it and had the logs hoisted to the top of the hill, too. These "Lincoln logs," as he jokingly calls them, would form the walls of what was to be his guesthouse. "This was never going to be the house I lived in," Lannie says, "but I moved in and said, I never want a guest overnight."

Lannie's voice is soft around the edges, like barely melting butter. And his eyes flash when he says this kind of thing because to know him is to know that he is every inch an extrovert, someone who draws energy and joy from being surrounded by people. But in this case, he is being serious. On this piece of land that he can't help but call "heaven," he found a place where he could relish being alone, at least for short increments of time. So ten years after building the cabin, he added a substantial addition and says, twisting his hand to indicate the enchanting space in which he stands, "This is my chateau in France now."

Lannie certainly has cause to say so. His front door opens into an expansive room that waxes regal from ionic capital down to polished parquet floor. The room's pronounced architectural elements, which at one time served as the setting for an exhibition of pieces from Versailles, now frame Lannie's own museum-quality art collection, with piece upon piece of art, each in gilded frame, climbing the richly colored walls. In the middle of it all, Lannie, like a wizard, flips a switch to reveal hidden revolving panels in the walls, including one that conceals a tiny, secret bedroom complete with leopard-print bedspread and nightstand. Prompting new visitors into guessing games about the origins of the spindles on his stairwell and the artist responsible for such-and-such painting, Lannie floats about his home with a whimsical delight that casts aside any notion that he is perhaps pretentious or intimidating. Lavish in style, certainly, but in character, he is jovial, welcoming, magical.

Lannie's art collection includes a rare Winslow Homer, but his favorite piece is a painting by the wife of a former professor.

A self-proclaimed "windbag," Lannie likes to tell the story about the night he completed the house, just shy of his 74th birthday. As he tells it, he called his son Matthew and his daughter-in-law, Allison, who also live on the property and said, "I want my birthday present tonight." When they said they didn't have anything for him, he insisted. "I was very demanding," Lannie says demurely. What he wanted was for them to come see his new addition. "As my son walked in, I saw his eyes, and I said, 'It is over the top, isn't it?' And he said, 'Well, what did you expect?'" At this, Lannie chuckles, eyes alight, before adding, "They don't like my lifestyle. They're very simple, minimalist people—and the more the better for me."

This is hardly a family secret, and Lannie makes the comment in their presence. It is a Sunday afternoon in early October, and he has retreated to the screened-in porch at the back of his house to visit with Matthew and Allison, who are enjoying time off from the arduous work that otherwise consumes their daylight hours. Organic farmers, they live and make a living on the property, whereas Matthew's older brother, Andrew, has settled in Nashville. "Andrew got his mother's brain," Lannie says, referring to his late wife Louise, who passed away when the boys were in their teens. "She was brilliant. And my oldest son is brilliant," he explains, telling how Andrew could remember telephone numbers from real estate signs he had seen years prior. Because Andrew is now a successful stockbroker, married with school-age children of his own, Lannie doesn't foresee him moving out to the country. So it is Matthew and Allison who share with Lannie in calling the land home, though for the time being they live in its valley as opposed to on its hilltop.

Their current house, which came with the purchase of a second parcel of adjoining land and which Lannie likes to call the "bastard house," is a study in disrepair: a temporary fix until the couple completes construction of their own house, sited high on the hill not too far from Lannie's. Despite the proximity, their house will be nothing at all like Lannie's. Their intention is for it to be "efficient" with a basic floor plan, an entirely solar-powered water system, and no central heat or air. "We're not trying to make a green house," Allison insists. "We just want to have something that you're living in that is appropriate, nothing wasteful. Nice but nothing wasteful."

The concept of nothing wasteful stands in stark contrast to Lannie's attitude of tasteful extravagance. In fact, much about Matthew and Allison Neal stands in stark contrast to Lannie Neal. Whereas Lannie thrives on an active social life, traveling into town four or five times a week to see friends, Matthew and Allison generally make only one trip into Nashville, for Wednesday deliveries and errands. Whereas Lannie delights in cooking

Typically the talker, Lannie sits back to listen as his daughter-in-law Allison and son Matthew tell of rescuing—amid dangerously rising floodwaters—the jar of savings they had buried in their garden.

and eating food of all forms, Matthew and Allison don't, as Matthew says, "partake of conventional fare." Whereas Matthew and Allison spend entire days outdoors, sifting through the dirt, tending to the unrelenting demands of farm life, Lannie tends to stay indoors when home, reading voraciously, working on a book project, and listening to classical music. He gets chiggers; they don't.

But for all of their differences, the love and mutual respect between them is palpable. They know how to treat each other lightly: Matthew rubbing his father's full stomach as a way of teasing him, for instance. Or Allison erupting into giggles at Lannie's joke that they could increase profits if only they would abort their organic practices and "just do it right."

However comfortable they are with teasing, they clearly understand the importance of taking each other seriously, too, of believing in the life's work that each has chosen. Though Lannie has no intention of working in the fields, he says with all conviction: "There are really only two noble professions in the world, one is teaching, like it used to be, and one is farming." And though Matthew and Allison view Lannie's tastes as extravagant, they celebrate him for the beau-of-the-ball that he is.

"He knows the way we are, and we know the way he is. We all appreciate the way we are," Allison explains, then adds: "But it's not as if we have crazy different beliefs. There are some underlying cores that we all share." This is the crux of the Neal family story. Despite the marked differences that might easily have distanced Matthew from his father or alienated Allison from her father-in-law, despite all the contrasts that might set the three at odds, there is a profound connection that instead draws them together. It is what brings all of them to call Leipers Creek Road home.

Marathoner

Allison was the last to join the Neals on the family farm, not marrying Matthew until almost ten years after Lannie bought the first of five total tracts of land, but in many ways, the farm is her baby. She is quick to say that Matthew was already growing a substantial garden when she met him, but Lannie is quick to rejoin that he thinks, "personally, if it were not for this gal, my son would not be here today doing what he's doing." Matthew agrees.

"Allison keeps us going," he says of his wife. "She is a marathoner. She has the ability to see it and to work toward it."

Allison is literally a runner—she raced long-distance for Belmont during college—and she looks it: tall, lean, angular. The endurance training she practiced during those years has served her well in a profession that requires exhausting manual labor twenty-eight weeks out of the year, the official seven-month season. But perhaps even more importantly, as

Matthew references, is how it cemented her dogged perseverance and far-sightedness.

This is how Allison has established a fully organic produce farm that has, in only a few seasons, successfully offered first a CSA (Community Supported Agriculture) and then an online store, while also selling to the local Whole

Allison shows Max, the farm's only full-time employee, how many stems of arugula to pick per bunch.

Foods. It was her idea to farm for the wider community, and it is she who runs the operations. In the fields, Allison directs the work, telling Matthew and their employee Max what to pick and where to plant, when to wash and how to arrange. As she explains, without arrogance or friction, "I'm the one that organizes everything. So if he [Matthew] was to do anything related to anything out in the field, he would have to hear it from me." She is typically the one to drive the tractor when necessary, and she is the one to keep the books, making detailed notations of the daily workings of the farm.

Allison's understanding of the science of farming is rooted in her study of chemistry and physics—she was at one point interested in medicine—but her feel for it, her general know-how and confidence, traces back much

further to when she was a little girl, the fifth generation, on her grandpar—
ents' farm. "I wasn't the child that was having to go out and get the eggs
in the morning," she says, explaining that her father had a "normal job."
So, rather than being subject to a list of chores, she could visit the farm
after school as a "floating person that got to kind of play and explore"
but most importantly, "to *see*." In seeing, Allison was learning.

From this personal history of apprenticeship, Allison has formed a clear
vision for the farm's future. Having interns has always been important to
Allison and Matthew because their mission is as much about outreach as
it is about production. They want to spread the word, encouraging people
to take ownership over food in a way that will reverse the unhealthy and
destructive trend of chemical engineering. Over the years they have had
an open-door policy for interns, inviting interested people to help in the
fields in exchange for a share of the harvest and a home-cooked lunch.
This year they went a step further, asking one of their most devout interns,
Max, a twenty-year old Nashville native interested in sustainable living, to
stay full-time.

Max, who now calls Allison and Matthew his "extended
family," lives on the property in a tent and works alongside
them during the day, usually barefoot, usually smiling. Max
is a testament to the Neals' internship program and eager
to say so: "I basically learned everything I learned out here.
The funny thing is I was working with them a few years ago
and that fall I went to MTSU because I wanted to study
agriculture. I stayed there for a semester, because I realized
I was really learning what I was learning about farming here."

It is this idea—of having people learn about farming by actually farming—
that Allison hopes to build on in the future. She and Matthew's vision is
of a non-profit program called "The Windfall Agrarian Initiative" that
would emphasize education through sharecropping. "This whole valley

along Leipers Creek is just so fertile," she explains. "We have plenty of the trace minerals, and then just the texture, the silty loam, it's the perfect agricultural medium. All these lands we have that are fallow, not being used, interns could start here, learn things they need to learn here," she says, "then eventually we could start working with other Land Trust land, kind of like a collaborative that we want eventually to be able to pursue."

The Windfall Initiative speaks directly to Allison's larger call to action. "It has to occur, or I don't see how civilization is going to continue. Meaning, I feel land is very important and growing food is very important, and I don't understand why that can't always be the center of everybody's—" she doesn't finish but tacks in a new direction. "Food and land just seem like they should always be the central core. If that could always be the central core, then it seems like everything else would just –"

"It's a bit of a utopia for the common time," Matthew ventures, serious but smiling. He knows Allison well. He knows that driving her intense work ethic and ambition is an unflagging optimism. And also an innocence, the combination of which makes her believe wholeheartedly in change and therefore cling even more fervently to their cause.

Allison's innocence is refreshing. In some ways, her life experiences have been sheltered: having come to Nashville from the Tri-Cities, the first time Allison ever flew on an airplane was to attend a track meet in college, an obvious juxtaposition to the world traveling that her husband and father-in-law have done. And yet, there is no resulting self-consciousness in her, no feeling of inferiority. Allison is Allison, fresh-faced and upbeat. She radiates an essential goodness, and this must have been part of Matthew's attraction to her.

All Around Windmiller

The two met one afternoon in a park. Allison was lying on a blanket reading a medical textbook; Matthew was looking for someone to throw Frisbee with him.

"All the sudden I feel someone come and tap my shoulder and I kind of look up," Allison tells, "and there he was. I thought he was awful cute and his hair was real curly," she says, tucking her chin away, a tide of

giggles edging forward. "So we threw Frisbee for a little while and then he was kind of like, 'Well thanks for throwing Frisbee. I guess I'll see you around town,' and he just was gonna—he just was gonna keep on! Say bye and see you later!" The laughter erupts now, heartily, as she divulges that it was she who suggested they exchange numbers.

When Allison talks about falling for Matthew, she reveals a great deal about herself as well as about the man who is now her husband. At twenty-three, Allison was in many ways naive and impressionable, infatuated with an older man who was unlike any she had met before. "I don't think I'd ever been around somebody that I felt was as interesting in thought or provoking in thought as maybe Matthew." At the same time, Allison was smart enough to understand the complexities of a guy who, as she says, "really didn't want to love anybody" and "really didn't want to be married possibly." Recognizing the risk involved in loving someone so free-spirited, she decided to pursue the relationship anyway, without trying to change him. And because of that, "It all worked out. He really did love me. But, um," she admits, blushing, "I just loved him a lot from the beginning."

When Allison met Matthew, he had already lived outside of Tennessee a number of times—including at boarding school in Connecticut and in Oregon in his early 20s, where he says he "didn't know anybody, didn't have anything other than my truck"—and he had saved enough airline points to go "wolfing" in Australia and New Zealand, essentially an exchange of room-and-board for farm labor. For seventy days, he had what he articulates as "that good experience of being younger and birds of a feather, running into people, having a nice time, seeing beautiful country, living primarily in the out of doors." These were the experiences of the free-spirited person with whom Allison was falling in love.

But Matthew was, and is, more than that. Introverted but genuinely interested in other people, brooding to a certain extent but at the same time jocular, Matthew is not a quick study. "A dreamer," his dad would say, but a thinker, too, at times a cynical one. Gentle but also physical, extraordinarily creative but mechanical, he and Allison like to joke that he is the farm's "all around windmiller."

"I endeavored into the windmill business for a little while," Matthew offers. It's hard to know whether to believe him because he deadpans masterfully. He claims he's telling the truth but leaves it to Allison to explain the label's real relevance: "It's just kind of like the end summation of somebody that comes and kind of does everything," she says, likening the windmill's circular shape to the fullness of his talents.

Drawn to "the slow process of invention and building," Matthew is personally engaged in the design and construction of his and Allison's new house.

"You know, the Don Quixote of sorts," Matthew chimes in, probably joking, but with an obvious grain of truth. He was the one responsible for engineering that nearly impossible task of bringing water up to his father's house and for designing the kaleidoscopic ceiling in his father's bedroom. He was the one to build the bridge across the creek, painstakingly smoothing out the turnbuckles in the old railway flatcar he used as the base. And he is the one who will build his and Allison's future home from the ground up with his own two hands. "Matthew can do it all," Allison explains. "He can do electrical, he can do plumbing. If you can do it, why would you pay someone to do it?" she asks rhetorically.

Having pored over the plans for providing water to his own house, Matthew has now broken ground on the project. He begins by digging water trenches. It is hard work he does high on the hill in a white shirt and pants. The attire is temperature-related but it gives Matthew a ritualistic, almost spiritual aura that suits him, because for all of his practical know-how, he is also an artist. He has been collecting fragments for years, discarded objects that he then uses to make one-of-a-kind light fixtures. Lannie and Allison both envision him doing more of this kind of creative endeavor in the future.

"Well, it's always nice to think that when you're seasonal, in the wintertime maybe I could do this," Matthew replies, "but there's always something else to be done because you just kind of have your nose on the stone." And the stone, for the time being, is the house, which Matthew is intent on making as chemical-free as possible.

Chemicals, and the state of affairs in the modern world at large, give Matthew cause for great alarm. When Matthew's brain starts to tick, it runs like a timer, sequentially honing toward a buzzer when a solid opinion has been formed. The timer runs like this: "There's a lot of things that I'll identify with in life that I really don't like. I look at the car and I think it's a hot day. The front of the car is the vent. The car

in front of me is a tailpipe, and what comes out of that tailpipe comes in through my vent, and you can smell it. And when I go into town to do delivery, and I come back, I always feel bad—physically bad—because of what I've picked up in town." The buzzer sounds, and the opinion is this: Matthew doesn't want to have to appropriate these "things that really just aren't agreeable" into his life. "Not that I want to be the system fighter," he clarifies. "I just don't want to smell the truck."

Allison chuckles at this diatribe of Matthew's. It is no doubt part of what attracted her to him, this man who was more "provoking in thought" than any she had met before. Matthew, in turn, seems to appreciate that Allison shares his views but is less worn down by them.

When he talks, no matter how impassioned by his topic, Matthew's pace is rarely aggressive or rushed. His voice is aristocratic-sounding with a warble so that "l" sounds roll under his tongue and never crisply surface. Typically very accurate in his diction, Matthew's vocabulary threatens to fail him when he shifts to talking about this bright-eyed woman whom he would in fact let himself love and marry.

"You know you hear the term salt of the earth and I guess that's just kind of – you just, you just feel one—and where you're comfortable is where you want to be and so that's where you are, and that's just what you do," he says by way of trying to explain his feeling for her. "I think we were too similar, really," he concludes. "We were just too similar." He adds these lines not as an indication of an incompatibility between them but as the exact opposite. He and Allison were too similar not to be together, not to make joint choices and move forward with shared convictions.

Companion Plants

Matthew and Allison married on an organic farm in Italy in 2007 with only close family attending, then returned to Tennessee to begin life, and work, together. Because marriage has also meant a partnership in running

Taped on the cabinet where Allison molds dough is a card with the words "Let us fly with love" handwritten around the border. In the middle she has written Matthew's name.

the farm, the two spend far more time together than a typical couple, and their shared philosophy about work becomes a shared philosophy about life. It is one that other people consider liberal but that Matthew and Allison consider very conservative.

"With our farming practices, we are extremely conservative," Matthew explains, drawing out the four syllables of the word sharply to give it emphasis. "When we talk to people who farm in the current methods with fertilizers, pesticides, and herbicides, they look at us and think we are extremely liberal. Organic farm: extremely liberal. But it's really an oxymoron because all of that to us is very liberal."

The same goes for their eating habits. Neither Allison nor Matthew will eat a single thing that is not 100%, down-to-the-last-ingredient organic, a decision that has provided them excellent health but limited their ability to socialize and travel. The couple has been known to bring their own food to dinner parties, which elicits all sorts of comments from more "liberal" eaters. "You know,

After the morning harvest, Max, Matthew and Allison gather beneath the hackberry tree that often passes as their dining room. They share slices of warm raisin bread and a hearty kale salad that Allison has prepared.

the little talk of the table is wow they brought their own food, how weird is that," Matthew says. "We're kind of tired of being the weird people, but at the same aspect, we're so glad that we can provide food that's nutrient-dense that's chemical free, and we always wonder why people aren't more concerned about what they're eating."

Though their strict dietary codes isolate the two of them, neither sees the choice as optional or problematic. "We're probably tying ourselves into a little tin," Allison admits in a tone more carefree than concerned. For Matthew, it's quite simple: "Well when you grow your own food, you have your own food so why would you want somebody else's food."

That is easy to say when your wife is a trained chef. Having worked at high-end restaurant Zola and then as a personal chef, Allison performs an understated magic in the kitchen. What happens there is a direct consequence of what happens in the fields. And a direct reward. Whatever is fresh and prime is what gets cooked, so Allison never follows or repeats a set recipe. She relies instead on her own creative combinations, like a recent arugula hummus that Matthew reported feeling "ecstatic about."

Lannie sentiments are similar. He calls Allison a "fabulous cook" and praises an apple galette she made for a recent party of his. Lannie is himself a cook and though the nature of his ingredients doesn't always match his daughter-in-law's, their love of well-prepared food is mutual. So is their pleasure in bringing people together to break bread, and it is this pleasure that has prompted Matthew and Allison's newest venture on the farm: open-air meals. Once a month, Allison fixes an all-organic, from-the-garden feast, which she and Matthew serve beneath the stars. The air outdoors, the robust flavors, the small size of the party, each of these factors enhances that critical feeling of intimacy that communal eating provides.

It's somewhat of a paradox that Allison and Matthew enjoy hosting meals but are generally unable to attend those given by others, even their own father, and yet, this is how they operate. They choose personal conviction over popular opinion and deal with the consequences, including relative seclusion. They are happy this way. They share a conservative life together: planting, planning, raising chickens, cooking, talking, and taking walks, especially during the winter when the woods afford a nice walkability.

In many ways, Matthew and Allison are like the companion plants they grow. The practice is one Allison learned from old Appalachian farmers, who through years of experience learned what plants to pair together because of the mutual benefits to the growth and health of each. Allison gives a few examples: rutabagas and peas, for instance, or marigolds and melons. "Some of it is scientific," Max points out, but some of it isn't. It's an old-fashioned wisdom that says one plant just thrives more fully with a certain other plant beside it. Such is the case with Allison and Matthew.

Lannie always sets his table the day before a gathering, taking care to add small touches that will heighten the sense of occasion.

Bell-Jar Roses

Lannie's explanation is more succinct: "They are two peas in a pod," he says merrily. Seeing his son happily married to a vibrant woman and having them here, living beside him, obviously bring Lannie a great deal of joy. Most of life seems to bring Lannie joy, which is no surprise because he chooses to live this way: "The one thing I told my children growing up is, it doesn't make any difference what you do in life as long as you enjoy it. Life just goes by."

It does, but for Lannie, not without a party. "I really enjoy entertaining. It's an unusual thing entertaining out here in the country. But I enjoy it," he reiterates. He tells of the Christmas following the completion of his new addition in 2009. "I didn't want everybody to come in at one time and say hello and walk out and say goodbye. I wanted to entertain my way, so I did!" He hosted a series of dinner parties: seven in a row, every other

night, with eighteen to twenty guests at each. His trick was having the same menu every night and a well-versed team of servers, but the key to his success is always his inimitable hospitality. And his attention to detail.

As Matthew says, Lannie is "a pleaser," one who can't help but outdo himself for the sake of others. This has made him not only a master entertainer but a master interior designer as well. He stumbled upon his vocation early. As a boy, he used to transform cardboard boxes into windows and doors and paint them. "I really always wanted to be an architect, I think," Lannie says, "but I was not math-inclined so I decided I would be a designer instead."

Over fifty years in the business and still loving it, Lannie laughs that he has more work now in retirement than he did when he had an office. "In fact every time I go to the bank I think I've robbed people. Why am I getting paid for doing this? I should be paying them for letting me do it because I enjoy it so much! Very fortunately I have a wonderful list of clients that have been lovely people that have almost been—," Lannie slows these last words, acutely aware of how fully he means them. "—like a part of the family. People have just so spoiled me in being nice to me. A little boy from Ferguson Avenue, my parents really never had anything, and I have been so —" he stops short, merriment giving way to profound gratitude, "so blessed. I've had a wonderful life."

Collecting himself quickly, Lannie elaborates on his upbringing. "My parents had absolutely nothing. They were poor as Job's turkey," he says with humor and without hesitation. But his father's mother originally came from a "very grand family" who at one time had "1000 acres from Broadway out to Antioch," and his father was able to spend his summers there. During that time, he became enamored with land, a quality he passed on to his son. "I used to love to play in the ground as a child," Lannie says. "My aunt lived right across from the Joy Floral Greenhouses, and they threw all these unbelievable roses away. And I would take them. I took them home and I put them underneath bell jars and developed rose plants, and I had a little rose garden. As a very young child."

At one point, Lannie's father tried to move them back to the ancestral farm, but when his mother found bedbugs, she threw a fit and refused to stay. It wasn't until his retirement from the police department that Lannie's parents bought a small farm of their own and moved there permanently. "My mother just loved it," Lannie says, almost whispering. "She thought it was the greatest thing she'd ever done. So when I got married—I married a girl from Northern Alabama who was a farm girl—"

"Rural," Matthew says, emphatically.

"Very rural," Lannie affirms. "Louise gave me the same ultimatum that my mother gave," announcing that while her sons were young, she would not be stuck living out in the country.

Lannie first met Louise at Satsuma, a restaurant downtown, where they were each dining alone. The hostess, who often sat people together to fill up a table, noticed them and decided to put them together. It was during that lunch that they, as Matthew says, "saw something in one another." It was during that lunch that Louise, in particular, saw in this vibrant man someone who could change the course of her life.

Sad Realities

"I always want to tell her story when someone asks me about my mom," Matthew says. "I have all the fragmented memories, and I have rolled them into a story. It's not a story," he corrects himself. "It's basically what I knew of her, where she came from, how things came to pass…."

"My mother grew up in Alabama," he begins, "extremely poverty-oriented. She was one of five children; she was the only girl and she was the youngest." He goes on to recount the fact that when Louise was only eleven, her mother died, forcing her to assume the role of matriarch as a young girl. "Her childhood wasn't so much a childhood," he suggests, explaining that when she had the opportunity to depart the country and live with an aunt in town, she jumped on it. "And so later on, when she and my father met, evidently, I think they saw something in one another."

Lannie and his late wife, Louise, in the early '80s.

At that point in time, Lannie had begun his career as a designer and Louise, as Matthew shares, "wanted to come up in life from what she was. Dad was, I guess, just starting to be successful. She wanted things in life she had never had," he says pointedly. "And that was an opportunity for her. And my father wanted children, which I guess he saw as an opportunity for him. This is *my* story," he is careful to say, before going on to share the details of his mother's eventual death, when she was in her fifties and he was fourteen, home on break from boarding school.

"This is really bizarre," he starts, slowly. "Dad and I were out. He was working and I was riding with him. And there's a four-way stop at Harding Place and very close to Belle Meade Boulevard. At that four-way stop, she was ahead of us. She had an old, big, heavy, blue Cadillac, and we came behind her. She turned right, and we turned left. Now we didn't honk," he tells, replaying the details of the exact location, the colors, the sounds, and the absence of sounds, in his head. "And that was the day she killed herself. It was just so odd to run into somebody at a stop sign and to be their wife and to be their mother and their son and their husband, and we didn't honk, which was really bizarre. When you see somebody you definitely honk, and that was the day that—"

Matthew breaks off from the story. He talks about being too young to understand any chemical imbalances that his mother may have had, or any medications that may have affected her negatively. He mentions a strange membership in a church, but for the most part, he lets it be. "I didn't really look for a lot of cause and effect of why. That's not my personality. It's what happened," Matthew says, frankly but not angrily.

Lannie's reaction is similar. "I didn't realize how bad it was until after she was gone. How bad it was for her, quite frankly." Lannie remembers it as a "sorrowful time for all of us," not a time marred by the need to place blame. Ultimately, he says, "what was done was done and that was it."

They built a small chapel on the hilltop to be her final resting place, but Matthew seems to visit her more intimately in a photograph he keeps in the desk drawer in the kitchen. "It's her, just at her prettiest, and she was a pretty woman," Matthew says fondly, holding her old passport from the '60s. The eyes of the woman in the photograph are Matthew's eyes: prismic, profound. "I can appreciate her struggles in life from what I know, and then having some of her obviously in me and struggles that I've had," he says.

Matthew doesn't elaborate on any particular struggles that would liken him to his mother, but his attitudes toward some things, like his discomfort with the "progress" of modern life and with certain romanticized notions of farming, do suggest an awareness of life's darknesses, whether inherited or learned.

When Matthew talks about life on the farm, and life in general, he discusses a notion he calls "the sad realities." "The sad realities are what my personality seems to always have to address and it seems like those are always the things that are left out of the romantic stories," he says. He uses culling chickens as an example. He raises heritage breeds, birds not manipulated by science whose lineages trace back to Spain, Denmark, and France, and he chooses to raise hens and roosters alike, despite the inherent difficulties. "It's our responsibility when roosters get to a certain age, they're going to kill each other or we have to kill them. I don't want to have to grab a bird by the legs and take them to their final place. But… there's an integrity involved, that quality to it that makes me feel better about getting up in the morning and culling chickens."

"Doing the part that not everybody can do," Allison says.

"Or wants to do," Matthew adds. "You try to find the good side of it," he says. "At least we can find motivation to do what we have to do because it is part of the cycle."

Respect for this cycle underlies the name he and Allison chose for their farm, Arugula's Star. When arugula flowers, it looks like white stars, a sight most people miss because they're only interested in the plant as food. "When vegetables go to flower, they're really beautiful and people never know what that looks like," Allison explains. "Somebody has to be letting that vegetable go to that point or you can't plant it again. That's part of being involved and getting to see a full season." She and Matthew are those people. They are the ones who understand the necessity of a complete cycle.

Fullness

The word Matthew lands on when he talks about the cycle is "fullness." It's a word that triggers an acute memory for him, one from years ago when he was waiting in the checkout line at Wild Oats and was struck by an image on a magazine cover. "The photograph was of an Asian elderly

man that was being held like this by his son," he shares, gesturing with his arms. "He was an elderly man and his son was probably about forty-five years old, and his son was holding him and he was his caretaker."

As Matthew recalls the details of the image, he processes the larger implications they now hold. Lannie is in his mid-seventies, and though he leads a vivacious life, he recently fell very ill with pneumonia. Refusing to go to the hospital for fear of further sickness, he retreated to his own bed,

coughing some nights from eight until one in the morning. During those times, Lannie admits to having prayed for the end.

Matthew comes back to the photograph as a way of articulating his emotions about his father's aging. "That one image, it really just stopped you and made you realize the beauty of a parent-child relationship. How it comes around from the child coming into the world, being raised, and then the flip side. The circle of it really was powerful."

Matthew wonders aloud whether he will have a strong enough sense of devotion to "rise to that occasion." While it's clear that he would, and will, Matthew's doubt is an honest way of acknowledging the tension he sees as inherent in parent-child relationships. Children feel compelled to prove themselves to their parents, he believes, and in the process push them away. "You push away until you learn when to push, when not to," he says. On his part, Lannie admits he's not so sure he was the "fatherly type." He was into his work, and he and Louise generally left the child rearing to a team of hired help. Both men acknowledge the many ways they differ. "My father has trouble putting in a light bulb. His weakness is my strength," Matthew states. "He's been a breadwinner and I have not. I didn't become the barrister."

Matthew might have ended there, but he doesn't. Trumping all the obvious differences is a closeness with his father that extends deep into his child-hood, well before his mother's death, he says. "We have an innate simi-larity, an obvious—almost something to do with the sun and astrology, some bond which makes us agreeable…Yes, similarities and also differ-ences, as are natural, but we've just always had that rapport. He and I, I think we've helped each other with different things. It's that constant, too," Matthew adds, "of him always being close by."

"Of course we have our differences," Allison ventures, "but we're all still connected."

Matthew knows this is true. In his bones, he knows. But he enjoys posing the question anyway: "*Why* are we connected?"

"Because of, well for you, it's family," she answers. "And now because I'm part of the family."

"It's because of the —," he says, pointing a slender finger downward.

"The land," she replies.

"The land," Matthew affirms, nodding.

"I sort of broke down when we were putting this place in The Land Trust," Lannie says, acknowledging that his family was sharply divided over the decision. "Finally, I said, 'We just need to do this and do it once and for all before I pass on.' And um. I think um…" Trying to continue, it seems as if Lannie might break down again. He takes a long pause to collect himself. "It's a very small thing," he manages. "But I think putting this 150 or 60 or 70 acres or whatever we've got is one of the best things I've ever done."

Dabbing at his eyes, Lannie can barely make it through the end of the sentence. The creaking of the porch, the gradual decrescendo from the classical music inside, and the soft rustle of the surrounding trees fill the unapologetic pause that follows his words.

"That's what I thought," Matthew eventually says, the soft words echoing his father's emotion.

Lannie leans in repose outside his front door, relishing the view of his land and the son who shares in calling it home.

Steve and Susan Fisher sing for their grandson, Judah, and their daughter, Holly.

The Fisher Family

Pretty Music

Sitting on the sofa, bare toes tapping, Steve Fisher eases his mandolin into tune.

He checks a note with his wife, Susan: "Is that too high for you?"

Susan's voice, spoken or sung, is a surprise: lilting and airy, as youthful as a child's. The Southern accent is not a drawl but crisp, and something about it calls to mind Nanci Griffith, a Grammy Award-winning folk singer who happens to be one of Steve's favorite musicians.

"We wore her out when we were fixing this house up," Steve says. "We had a cassette tape and played her all the time. I love her." It is a simple, direct statement delivered as such, without being overly emphatic. Steve is passionate and knowledgeable about a variety of things, from Eastern Highland Rim geography to bluegrass jam sessions, but his enthusiasm comes through always as authentic, never as overbearing. This, along with an easy sense of humor and a hint of mischief, makes him immediately likeable.

"I can't do that *Arggh*, that growl that she does," Susan says, picking up the Nanci Griffith comparison with a laugh that is like her voice, high and clear.

Susan grew up singing with her sister, Alice, the two harmonizing around their mother, who carried the central melody. She later learned to play her great-grandfather's fiddle, but for the most part, she is content to sing and

Portraits of her great-great grandparents look down on Susan as she plays the old family fiddle.

let Steve be the one to break out the instruments. Having played guitar for years, he is a mandolin convert and a singer in his own right. And when the two join voices, it's a simple, easy merging that explains how they have come to this moment: thirty-four years married, twenty-three of them living in this historic home on Susan's ancestral farm in Williamson County, just tapping time and singing harmony on a glorious Sunday afternoon.

Life for the Fishers is pure in this way but hardly effortless. Monday through Friday they both work "regular" jobs—he as the principal at Bethesda Elementary School, she as the librarian at the local branch. Evenings and Saturdays they work the farm, which entails taking care of their sheep, tending to the pastures at the front of their property, looking after the wildlife preserve at the back, and maintaining a vegetable and fruit crop substantial enough to supply their own table and feed members of the community as well. On Sundays, though, the Fishers slow down, devoting the day to being rather than doing.

"Every year when school starts, we recommit to each other that Sunday is a day of rest," Steve says. "We don't plant. We just hang out. Sometimes we'll do media fasts," he adds. "Go to church, come in, don't turn anything on, just read or nap or whatever."

Today, Steve and Susan rest by making music together. Their daughter, Holly, has brought their first and as-of-yet only grandson, Judah, for a visit, and the six-month-old seems as delighted with the activity as his grandparents are. It is the first time he has heard his grandfather play, and he can't help but coo and bob to the rhythms he is hearing. Susan can't help but coo and bob in return, as she kneels on the floor beside him, holding his dancing hands. Judah is the ninth generation of Fishers to be on the farm: an incredible legacy that is carried on, epitomized even, in this simple moment.

Picking crisp, sweet notes from the mandolin, Steve begins the lyrics of a Christian hymn, one that seems equally as fitting for his and Susan's faith as it does for their life together on the farm. "*I come to the garden . . .*" he begins in a low, gentle voice, and Susan picks up the lyrics high and bright on the next word: "*alone.*" Neither reflects the irony of a duet begun on the word "alone" as they continue to sing, their voices twirling one another naturally. But the meaning of the last line is not at all lost on the Fishers: it is the truth they live out daily as they go about their life's work. "*The joy we share as we tarry there,*" they sing together, "*none other has ever known.*"

They repeat the line, holding onto "*known*" in harmony, and then Susan turns her attention quickly back to Judah while Steve exaggerates the song's end with triumphant strumming and a smile for his grandson. The baby boy is the focal point of their afternoon and clearly the object of their affection. "Are you amazed?" she asks Judah gently. "You look like it. Goodness, goodness, that's pretty music," she says, taking up his hands again.

Growing On Each Other

Susan and Steve first started hanging out at the local pool when Steve was still in junior high and Susan, one year his elder, was already in high school. They fell into the same crowd, if not into love at first sight.

"I saw her," Steve tells. "I saw her and I think it was maybe, well, I don't know if it was love, but it was real interest in that first summer we met."

"We kind of grew on each other, I guess," Susan says with a laugh.

But Steve clearly remembers the moment he saw her: really saw her. "At a football game that fall, she and her friends were standing there, you know, and I was just kind of walking along and she was real fixed up nice." Susan giggles at the story, as if once again that bashful teenage girl. "Like real straight hair," Steve continues, "and she had on, like, an ultra-suede jacket and jeans." He drags out the word "ultra-suede" to poke a little fun at Susan and engender a laugh from his daughter.

"Is the story true," Holly asks, "about you showing up at Nana and Papa's house with a little bouquet of flowers, saying 'Is Susan home?'" It is clearly a sweet story of their courtship that has been passed on to their children.

Steve nods at Holly, letting Susan be the one to elaborate: "He used to have a little motorbike and he would come over on his motorbike, 'cause it was how many miles? Five or six miles away." Susan's parents assumed the relationship would be short-lived because the couple was so young, but Steve and Susan dated all through high school and married the following year, in 1978.

"I had a ponytail before we were married," Steve divulges, "but I did cut it off. My grandmother kept saying 'Cut your beard off, cut your beard off,' and I'd say, 'I'll trim it but I'm not going to cut it off.'"

"You have been teased about that so much over the years. You probably wish you had," Susan jokes with him. "Because when people see our wedding pictures, they're like who is that!" They both laugh, Steve leading the way. He clearly doesn't care that he didn't cut his beard, nor does she. Their relationship was, and continues to be, based on something far more significant: love, of course, and a shared desire to live in touch with the land.

Back to the Land

"We started dating fairly young…but we knew we wanted to have a farm one day," Steve says. "That was the big thing in the early to mid-'70s when people were leaving urban areas and going back. They were doing a lot of homesteading—that's what people called it—where they were going back and, you know, trying to get rid of all modern conveniences."

"We were '70s kids and that was after the hippies," Susan adds. "But definitely the back-to-the-land movement was still big, and we wanted to come out to the farm."

The farm in reference was Susan's family's farm, one bought in 1848 by her ancestors when they came westward from North Carolina. The land was worked and passed on through the generations eventually to Susan's great-grandparents, Lycurgus and Alice McCall, and then to her grandparents, Herbert and Mildred McCall, who lived on the farm when Susan was a little girl.

Mildred, known to Susan as "Mimi," was from one of the original families that settled in the area, as was "Granddaddy" Herbert, the only child of "Curg" and Alice. Smart and a bit spoiled, Susan suspects, Herbert was sent to school at Battle Ground Academy, which was atypical for the time. The story goes that Alice saved her egg money to send him there. The investment paid off because Herbert went on to college to become a teacher, but when the Depression hit, he was forced to quit and return to the farm to help. It was then that he met Mildred and married her.

Though he never returned to finish his formal education, he did go on to become a teacher and principal at the local school while continuing to run the farm—an uncanny parallel to the dual responsibilities that now, decades later, Steve carries on the same farm.

Susan's great-grandparents, Lycurgus and Alice McCall, with their son Herbert c. 1910.

Susan's memories of the farm jump immediately to the enthralling story of the farming accident that nearly took Herbert's life in 1962, when Susan was just four years old. He had been out working alone in the barn "chopping solid" with a wood-splitting machine that quit running. "He got mad at it and kicked it, which is very Granddaddy," she chuckles. "And it started. And it grabbed him, pulled him off his feet. It cut off his toes, both feet…It would have chopped him up all the way, gradually all the way—but he reached back and he was just able to grab the handle and turn it off."

Susan tells this story calmly without dramatizing. It's the way she tells most things about the farm—meeting things squarely as they are, not prone to exaggeration or romanticism. This may be part of the natural wear that farming can have on a person's attitude. But it may also be a remnant of the steadfastness that characterized her Granddaddy, who had to drive himself to the hospital that day and who continued to live and work the farm twenty-plus years after the accident, in shoes made specially for him. "His balance was always off quite a bit," Susan recalls, "but he always walked."

Susan has other memories, too—of Granddaddy tying strings around the legs of bumblebees and handing them to her to "fly" and of building playhouses out of hay bales up in the barn lofts. "My sister and I, we were outside all day," Susan reflects. "I remember being barefoot most of the time. Filthy feet. I'm sure we were filthy from head to toe, but we had not the slightest care about that." Susan marvels that kids today, as young as two or three, shriek to get their feet dirty. "Kids should be out playing, getting dirty all the time, but they don't anymore…Oh chiggers. Poison ivy. We experienced all of them, and we didn't care. Part of farm life," she notes succinctly.

Steve also grew up accustomed to farm life. Both sets of his grandparents lived out in the country, so he always had a place to go experience the outdoors. "Fished with one grandfather and hunted with another. I always liked that," he quips. This kind of rural living resonated with Steve as profoundly as it did Susan. Because of his interest in ecology and conservation, he intended to go into Parks and Recreation but had to change plans when Susan became pregnant with their first child, Travis, who now lives in Louisville and studies archaeology. Steve says that as a kid, Travis was always outside, finding Native American spearheads in the creek and foraging for things to add to his collection.

This is exactly what Susan and Steve had envisioned when they joined the back-to-the-land movement. "It's just beautiful. It's beautiful out here—the peace and quiet," Susan says, but what she has cherished most has been "just the opportunity for my children to be raised this way."

The Old House

Their daughter Holly admits that she wasn't always keen on living out in the country. "I didn't like living out here in high school, you know, because it was far away from all my friends. It was a thirty-minute drive everywhere I wanted to go, so I didn't like that. But I have good memories, too," she says, as her parents huff and chuckle.

"Well good," Steve says sarcastically.

Susan and Steve relish this weeklong visit from their daughter Holly, who now lives in Knoxville with her husband and the baby.

"We got our own Christmas trees for awhile," Holly says, telling how the four of them would climb into the pick-up truck to hunt the perfect one, never bothering to bring along a tape measure. "Oh, it's painted over—" she says, looking up at the ceiling. "Recently the ceilings were painted, but for a long time there was a scrape where…"

The three of them plunge into laughter as Holly tells the story of the Christmas tree that far exceeded the height of the living room ceiling. "It was too big, so dad brought the chainsaw inside!"

"No, I took it out twice," Steve corrects, "And on the third time, I closed the doors and opened that door, and cranked the chainsaw." Opening the door, Susan assures, was no help. In an instant, the room was full of smoke and shavings.

It is a room, a house in general, that figures prominently in many of the family's memories. The structure was originally a log cabin built in the late 1700s, and over the years, it has been covered up and added onto with the passing generations. The most significant renovations were done by Susan's great-grandparents, Curg and Alice. Alice had been given the farm as a wedding present from her father in 1898, and the couple began renovations soon thereafter at the turn of the century. Alice passed away when Susan's father was a boy, but Susan does have snapshot memories of Curg, whom she calls "Pap." In her mind, he sits on the hearth in the very room where the Christmas tree will scrape the ceiling so many years later, a jar of King Leo candy on his knee and eyes so translucent blue they "looked like they might be blind."

Sitting by that fire, Pap passed on stories of the farm and house, but a lot of what Steve and Susan know comes from their own renovations, which they undertook in February of 1988. They began by coming out on the weekends to clear the yard, but by the time they had hired a contractor and were more fully engaged in the project, they found a lot of their own clues about the house's story.

"Part of the front addition to the house is pre-Civil War," Steve explains. "We know that just because of the parts of it that I tore off…

And when we were running electrical here," he says, "we'd pull off weatherboard so we could feed wire through, and I found a board that was signed by a carpenter in Chapel Hill, 1901."

Susan admits that she was reticent to change the house in any drastic way and that their renovations, which included adding a bathroom, were difficult for her. "My thought was I didn't want to change the old house, but I had to end up making changes. There was just no way…But now, as long as we've been here, the house is associated with memories from our own small family as much as it is, for me, from my grandparents."

Holly was only three at the time the family moved in, so she doesn't remember helping paint the exterior of the house that first year, but for Susan, that memory among so many others is "just a little part of the history now."

Trial by Fire

Also part of the history is that first summer the Fishers spent in the house, when Steve and Susan faced the immediate consequences of their decision not to add central heat and air.

"Well, the very first—you know what I'm thinking of…" Susan says with a knowing look and laugh toward her husband. "The very first week that we moved out here, it was in June and there were record breaking temperatures…It was 100 degrees every day for a week. This was June!" she emphasizes.

"Nine o'clock at night and I'm just soaking wet," Steve says, remembering how he worked like a dog to get the screens secured on the porches. "I mean we had lights but it was a goal: if I could get the screen on, then I could open the doors."

"And it cooled down after that," Susan says, but then tells how, because of the heat, the spring went dry. The Fishers do have a tap for city water at the end of their drive, but they opted, and continue to opt, for natural spring water. That first summer, Steve had to haul in water using a 700-gallon tanker truck to fill the spring box until the rains came again.

Apparently, the test of will continued when the Fishers discovered, during the first cold snap, that their furnace wasn't going to work.

" If I could find those pictures," Steve says laughing. "If I could find that picture of me standing in my cowboy boots in front of the fire—"

"I know!" Susan erupts, catching Steve's energy and growing a notch more boisterous in the storytelling before settling back into its facts. "We didn't have the woodstove yet and we just had this furnace and it was on propane and it just kept burning up the propane like crazy. But it was never warm because the windows are old and the doors have big cracks around them," she explains with laughter still trailing.

The Fishers eventually got a woodstove, which continues to be their main source of heat, and Steve says he enjoys chopping firewood, at least until February when spring "can't come fast enough." They also continued to live without air conditioning, save window units in the kids' rooms, until only recently. "I probably wouldn't have gotten them, but Steve said, 'We just need to get air conditioners,' and he just went and got them," Susan explains. "It just seemed unnecessary to me, but I wanted to keep him happy. So, he is happy."

"Having an old house can be challenging," she summarizes. "Just because it's cold in the winter, it's hot in the summer, and there's usually something that needs to be fixed." But, as far as Susan and Steve are concerned, it's a small price to pay for a place so rich in personal history.

Sheep Farming

Raising sheep was not in the Fisher's original vision for the farm. Steve, who now leases some of their land to a local cattle farmer, had intended to raise cows himself. But a confluence of events, including a project at the kids' school that had Travis and Holly learning how to care for lambs, altered the plan for good.

At first, the sheep were more or less pets, with names like "Blossom" and "Miss Chickabee," but as the flock grew, those intimate relationships gave way to increased responsibilities. Steve is quick to point out, though, that sheep require less daily hassle than cows, which is one reason why he and Susan have continued to raise them this long. The sheep feed only once, in the evening, and most of the work is, as

Susan and Steve lure the ewe and her newborn triplets back to the safety of the barn.

Steve says, "maintenance," entailing breeding in the cooler months of fall and shearing in the warmer months of spring.

From October until December, Susan and Steve separate the ewes into breeding groups, each with an assigned ram, and then after the five-month gestation period, they begin looking for lambs. Though neither says so outright, the lambing season is obviously a highlight. "When they're little, they like to get on that concrete pad over there and jump off," Steve says, pointing to a fenced-in area by the barn. "We call it 'Lambie Games,'" he says, smiling. Susan echoes, commenting on how playful the lambs are and applauding how good the sheep are as mothers.

The nursing period, though, is brief, and the lambs are pretty quickly moved into a separate pasture. When Steve enters the gate to feed them,

the four-month-olds spook, dashing back and forth, bumping into one another, and ultimately getting confused as to how to navigate toward the feeding troughs. Steve just laughs at them, pointing out the ringleader who initiates the tizzy every time.

The older sheep are far more sedate though no less interested. Rather than scamper about, they stand, every last one, transfixed by Steve's approach. Undoubtedly they are hungry and expectant, but there is something both curious and trusting in the way they watch him. Only when he tosses out their hay do they jostle and bleat at him and one another, vying for the supper he has brought them.

Going about this chore, after a full day navigating the demands of school leadership, Steve shows no signs of fatigue or irritability. He and Susan have recently "down-sized," reducing their flock from fifty to fourteen, and in turn reducing some of the stress regarding their care. Though the change has meant less responsibility in some regards, such as less feeding during these evening rounds, it has actually meant more in others. Before, when the Fishers owned more sheep, they hired a guy to do the shearing, someone whose grandfather had been in the business before him. But with a reduced flock, Steve has taken on the job of shearing himself.

It is not easy, and Steve doesn't have a lot of extra time to do it, but he admits with a smirk playing slightly in his face, "I can be a bit on the compulsive side." This is coming from a man who ran five marathons in three years before he blew out his knee and had to quit. This is coming from a man who helped shear fifty-two sheep in one year—as a side-job.

That particular year was back when the Fishers had a large flock and were selling the fleeces for profit. Once the sheep were sheared, the fleeces then became Susan's responsibility, as she was the one to clean them in a process called "skirting." Spreading the fleece across her lap, she would pick it clean, readying some of it for presentation at the state fair and some for sale at auction. Susan could make skirting look therapeutic, the way she sat on the front porch, her fingers working meticulously and seemingly mindlessly, but she admits that it was in fact "back-breaking" and sometimes painful, depending on the amount of burrs embedded in the fleece.

The Fishers chose their particular breed of sheep precisely for the beauty of its fleece. And because it is a rare, old-fashioned breed that originated in, and is named for, the Cotswald hills of England.

Sitting on the front porch in the fall, Susan begins cleaning the wool in a process called skirting.

"This is especially good fleece," Steve says, pulling bag #215 from among the stacks in the old smokehouse where he and Susan store their wool. "This Cotswald is so open, some of the people buy it because they make doll hair... It's what makes the Santa Claus beards."

Fingering the thick fleece, Steve brags about his wife's prize-winning work, and she reciprocates by complimenting his progress with learning how to shear. Sheep-farming for the Fishers is clearly a two-person enterprise, and, as the sheep stand sentinel along the drive up to the Fisher's house, clearly part of the farm's visual and functional identity.

Pumpkin Patch

Susan and Steve both agree that spring is their favorite season on the farm: the time for Lambie Games as well as for gardening. Despite the fact that both Steve and Susan work full-time jobs, they have managed to have a garden every year since they moved out to the farm, save that first summer when they were still busy getting the house and the grounds ready.

Now, the garden is as much of a community affair as it is a family one. The Fishers have begun a small CSA, inviting members either to pick for themselves or to gather their weekly share in full or half bushels. And they have forged an alliance with a Bhutanese refugee group, inviting them to farm a small section of land for free through a program called Hope Rise.

Having originally fled Bhutan, this group of refugees spent as long as fifteen years in camps in Nepal before the UN, working through Catholic Charities, helped transfer them to places with more opportunity, like Nashville. But, as Steve points out, the older members who once held a place of honor in their society languished for lack of work. "When they came here, they sat in their apartments all day," he says. "It was freezing in their condos because they didn't know how to turn their thermostats on. Very few spoke English."

"A lady at our church somehow found out about them, and the idea sprang up for them to be able to garden and supply their community and hopefully sell," Susan explains. Recognizing their unique ability to help, the Fishers jumped to join the project.

That first visit, a chilly but vibrant day in mid-March, a group of nearly thirty Bhutanese men and women poured out of the various vans that had transported them to the Fisher farm. Dressed in a combination of brightly colored "kiras" and American-made sock hats, some in flip-flops, others in tennis shoes, they were bright-eyed, eager, and entirely unable to speak English. So they moved in clumps as Steve directed them—with the help of an interpreter but mostly through gestures and encouraging smiles—how and where to plant their rows. Which, as it turns out, they already knew.

"They didn't tell me they already knew how to farm out of courtesy," he says. "I thought I was really showing them how to plant, but I found out later they already knew how to do it." He recalls how they just laughed and smiled at him rather than becoming defensive or testy. "They are such sweet people," he notes, his own kindness rising to match.

The day was festive if not entirely successful. Their crop did not yield, mostly because of logistical problems involving transportation after that initial planting. Without drivers' licenses, the Bhutanese elders were unable to return to the farm with enough regularity to weed and tend to their crop.

Regardless, the Fishers invited them to try again, and they did, opting the second time for pumpkins instead of potatoes. Steve and Susan worried because the immigrants planted their seeds during the hottest, driest part of summer. And because it was a day when both Steve and Susan were working and unable to help supervise, they ended up planting them too close together. But, Susan says with a suggestion of providence: "Good rains came, and it really brought those pumpkins out."

And now, in addition to the fall crop that the Fishers have themselves grown—snow peas, broccoli, cabbage, Swiss chard, and kohlrabi, to name

Steve welcomes the Bhutanese refugees with a smile and a bag of onion sets, showing them where they can begin planting.

a few—they also have a field of pumpkins belonging to the Bhutanese. At first glance, the crop looks like another round of failure. But hidden beneath a canopy of rough leaves, there lay dozens of plump pumpkins, most still green but a few already brightening to their festive orange.

The Fishers are unsure of how and when the Bhutanese will return to harvest their crop, and they worry that the distance between their apartments and the farm is an insurmountable problem, but they remain open to the project and the prospect of helping. It is not a perfect system, but it is a generous and humble one, much like the Fishers themselves.

Bag End

Barreling down the driveway on his way home from work—windows down, *The Eagles* turned up—Steve says he can feel a shedding. That leisurely Sunday with family has given way to a Monday of chores and challenges, but coming home still has the power to right the world. "It's like no matter what happens during the day, when I turn on that road up there, everything starts to fall away, ya know." It is this feeling—of a place at the end of the road where everything else falls away—that he and Susan cherish and want to protect.

Steve slows at a juncture in the driveway where the curving gravel stops at a cattle grate. An old rectangular slab of wood hangs there, a sign, with the words BAG END FARM cut out of it in capital letters. Susan chose this name for the farm from a book, *The Lord of the Rings*, one of her favorites. It is the name of Bilbo Baggins' home: not a farm per se, but a cozy hamlet, old-fashioned and set apart from the bustle.

The spirit of the name carries Steve down the rest of the drive, to where Susan greets him on the front porch. There are chores but Daylight Savings hasn't yet turned the lights out on late afternoon, and so there is still time. Steve pulls on a t-shirt and grabs his walking stick. Susan

sprays for chiggers and props open
the door for the cats. They leave
the sleepy sheep dogs, Sarah and
Bonnie, to watch the flock, and the
two of them take a walk.

They head out from the back of the
house where two steep hills form
a natural pathway down the hollow.
Steve has recently learned that this
path used to be one of the old
buffalo traces, where herds of wild
bison used to run and where Native
Americans followed. Now, it is their
own private trail, one that takes
them back toward a high ridge and
a beautiful hidden pond. In winters
past, the pond has sealed ice tightly enough for the kids to skate. In fall,
it harbors clinging mists in the morning that, by afternoon, have lifted to
showcase color-laden reflections.

At one end is a sweetgum, giant and indefatigable. A few years ago,
beavers worked at the bark on the bottom, but the tree bled itself
profusely until its black sap had sealed up the wound from illness and
insect. Susan remembers the tree from when she was a little girl fishing
this back pond with her grandfather and a cane pole. "We'd always sit
under that sweetgum after we were done and eat. Eat candy," she says,
warmed and almost surprised by the immediacy of the memory.

Pressing on, she and Steve climb a steep hill and stop to turn back around.
When trying to decide where to build the family cemetery, they walked the
entire farm looking for the right spot and found it here, where the hills
curve in on all sides like an embrace, and the views are forever protected.

"We like this spot because when you look out, there won't ever be anything developed out there, as far as you can see," Steve says, referring to the conservation easement they put on their land almost ten years ago.

The Fishers aren't sure whether their own children will move here, as both are entrenched in life in other cities, but they have laid out a ten-acre envelope for them if they decide they want it. Holly says she and her husband have discussed the possibility, knowing that they would never be able to buy land like this on their own. "It's really a gift that we have this land already that we could build on if we like," she says. Or that Judah could someday, if he so chose.

"It's not that it's specifically for Travis or Holly, but there's just this possibility of these two building sites," Susan explains. "It could be a grandchild someday that wants to do that, like we did, you know, came back…. But with The Land Trust, we know that at least the farm will stay a farm even if it has to pass from our keeping it to someone else's."

The Fishers see their farm as a resource not only for their children and grandchildren but for all future generations, whom they fear will be facing a paucity of farms. "We see so few farms are left in this county, and I think it's just gonna continue everywhere, so that there's few that are left to be a really valuable resource."

"I think the farm is especially valuable in that it was her family, Susan's family tradition to never cut timber commercially…That big grove of trees, right there," Steve says, pointing his walking stick outward. "It all the sudden stands out because it's a north-facing slope…They're all just huge," he says, referring to the hardwoods growing there. That ridge, with its creek bed at the bottom, marks the division between the front part of the property, which is in pasture, and the back part, which is wildlife habitat.

The wildlife habitat is an important piece of the farm for the Fishers, as much a part of its value as a resource as the untouched stands of native oak and poplar. Steve does permit hunting there, but for the most part, the area is a safe haven for all manner of wildlife: deer, turkey, quail, rabbits, coyotes, raccoons, even bobcats. Though some of these animals can be a threat to their lambs, both Susan and Steve feel that it is important to allow them to thrive in their natural habitat.

The same goes for native grasses. One of Steve's missions for the farm is to kill off the fescue and timothy and rye grasses that have been planted and to re-establish the area's native grasses. Steve purposely lets some fields grow goldenrod and milkweed, plants other people commonly disdain, and he has successfully re-introduced a stretch of river cane along the creek bottom, but he wants to do more.

Steve always wants to do more. As if it is not enough to raise sheep and grow food for the community, protect wildlife and foster native plant growth, Steve has other ideas about how to use the farm for good, like hosting outdoor recreational programs for kids during the summers. "These are all my retirement projects," he says, smiling. Tilting his head in Susan's direction, he adds: "She'll tell you, I'm an idea guy. And the rule is, whatever idea you have, don't quit your day job!" he says, laughing heartily.

But he is serious when he reflects on what the farm has meant to him and his sense of purpose. "I couldn't imagine what I would do now if we lived in the suburb," he says. "I mean what would I do when I got home?" he asks incredulously and genuinely. This time it is Susan who laughs heartily. This is the man she married, one who, except on Sunday, isn't much for sitting down. "It's just good therapy," he replies. "There's always something to do."

Susan acknowledges that the surplus work of the farm can take its toll. "It's just adding more work to your routine," she says, "But if you love the place, which I do, I love it—so," she pauses just a blink, then states simply: "I wouldn't want to live anywhere else."

As Steve crooks his arm naturally over her shoulder, she slips hers easily around his waist. Not usually demonstrative, not usually leisurely, the Fishers allow themselves this moment together as they walk up the last hill toward home, a harvest moon rising elegantly above them.

Three generations of women—Vadie, Vicki and Mama V—walk the loop around their Sumner County property.

The Pierce Family

The Three Vs

The three Vs—Vadis, Vicki, and Vadie—sit in the living room making flowers out of brightly colored tissue paper. Vadie is cross-legged on the floor, while her mother and grandmother, whom they call Mama V, are tucked inside armchairs. Through the room's bay windows, the women can see out onto Old Hickory Lake, where johnboats of fishermen cluster along the banks of their property despite the day's gray chill.

The sight triggers a memory for Vicki, and an easy teasing begins. She brings up an old boyfriend of her daughter's, "the boyfriend who never did anything right." His one chance to redeem himself—by catching a prize catfish in that spot—he apparently botched.

"When he told us he caught it, we said, 'Well what did you do with it?'" Vicki tells. "He said he took a picture and put it back. We said, 'At least you could have brought it in so that we could fry it up!'" She unleashes her distinctive cackle: it is sudden and hearty and genuine. Vadie joins right in, and Mama V smiles. This is not a house where feelings get easily, and unnecessarily, hurt. These three know each other too well for that. They also know that good cheer is a better use of energy than injured pride.

They talk on, reminiscing about the trips the three of them used to take every summer, leaving husbands and fathers behind. Mama V recalls their bicycle trip around Lake Victoria in Canada, and Vicki revisits their whirlwind European tour when Vadie was only five. "I tried to do all of Europe in, like, a month," she shares as her mother nods, eyebrows raised. "It was a killer, killer schedule. So we morphed down into going

It became a tradition for the three Vs to take a girls' trip every summer, including this visit to British Columbia in 1987.

to Paris and renting an apartment and pretending like we lived there. That's when we started calling ourselves the three V girls."

Memories like these are bantered back and forth as the three generations of hands fold and bunch tissue. The carpet between them is already an impressive pile of orange, red, and purple blossoms—creations that will be used as centerpieces at Vadie's upcoming wedding to take place here on the family property, just as her parents' wedding did.

Of course, Vadie is not marrying the boyfriend who couldn't do anything right; he is long gone. She is marrying a fellow Nashvillian, though the two fell in love in Brooklyn, where they live. They will say their vows at the point just down from the house near the water's edge, where an old stump is flanked by sweetgum and redbud trees. The location is already a hallowed one because it is here, as along the path that traces the perimeter of the property, where Daddy Don's ashes are spread and his life honored.

"Daddy Don" Pierce was Vadie's grandfather and Vicki's father and Mama V's husband, a country music entrepreneur *Billboard* magazine once named "Country and Western Man of the Year." He was also the man who bought this land and named it Shawnee Waters.

"He loved to name things," Vadie says with a mix of nostalgia and delight. "He was the namer."

"And Shawnee Waters was just a good name," Vicki points out. "I can't say the Shawnee Indians were actually here."

"But he would say that just to make the story better!" Vadie says, laughing.

The mention of Daddy Don has caused all three sets of eyes to take on a certain glow. It is obvious that the 3 Vs' love of the land is rooted in their love for this man and that it is his legacy that they joyfully, reverently preserve.

The Legacy of Daddy Don

Literally born on his mother's kitchen table, Don Pierce grew up in Seattle, the place where he and Vadis Larrabee originally met. He was an Army officer stationed at Fort Lawton, and "Lari" as he would affectionately come to call his wife was working there.

Mama V laughs, with just the slightest hint of indignation, when she tells the story of meeting Don's mother. Mrs. Pierce was skeptical of this unknown beauty from South Dakota, a girl ten years her son's junior with an exotic-sounding name, so she invited Vadis to her house for what was clearly a once-over.

Don Pierce and Vadis Larrabee posed for their engagement photo in 1942.

"His mother had this little retreat out at Lake Washington," Mama V tells. "She was a big Catholic, and she invited me over—unbeknownst to Don— to interrogate me. He came home unexpectedly and said, 'What're you doing here?' And I said, 'Your mother invited me. I didn't think I could hardly turn her down!'" This is Mama V's own story, before the time of her daughter and granddaughter, and she tells it with enunciated confidence before letting their laughter merge with and overtake her own.

The story's ending is obvious: Vadis passed the test. She and Don married. The two of them then lived in Don's mother cottage before eventually moving to California. There, in L.A., Don began the career path that would eventually bring him and his wife and their only daughter, Vicki, down South. Freshly discharged from the Army, Don cashed in his war bonds to buy shares in an unknown recording company called All Star Artist Bureau. Before long, he found himself having lunch with Woody Guthrie at a local joint called Melrose Grotto and publishing some of the era's first Country and Western hits. Don was so often in Nashville on business that the couple decided to move their life there.

Vicki laughs about her father's tricks to get her to agree to leave her friends and move to Tennessee. "He said, 'I know you love living in California, but there are things you can do in Tennessee that you can't do in California. If you embrace this move, I will buy you a dog and I will buy you a horse,' and there was no looking back after that!" she laughs.

Settling just outside of Nashville in Sumner County, the Pierces immediately made good on their promise to their daughter, buying her a German Shepherd she named Bimbo and a Quarter Horse she named Blue.

"It's like the Obamas," Vadie interjects, getting a giggle out of her grandmother to match her own. This quick wit is typical of Vadie and Vicki and, more subtly, Mama V. They are always bolstering each

Behind where Vicki and Mama V sit chatting is a sculpture made of cascading fuchsia flowers, one of the many works of art by Vadie that enliven the house.

other and the moment; with them, no topic is too sacred for a crack of laughter.

Vicki goes on to tell the story of staying awake all night to help Blue through an intense labor and delivery. It's a memory that obviously brings her a great deal of joy, both for what she loved about the horse and for what she loved about her father, who was less than pleased when the school called to report that his daughter's absence would result in her receiving all Fs for the day. His response, as she recalls it, went something along the lines of "She has learned more about life in this one night than she could ever learn at your damn school." As the story goes, the head-mistress apologized effusively to Don before granting his daughter an excused absence.

Don's record label, Starday, was known for its eye-catching LP jackets, including this 1966 album by signed artist and friend Minnie Pearl.

Mama V recalls that to even send her daughter to Harpeth Hall was difficult because of the long commute from Hendersonville into Green Hills in the days when there was no I-440 to expedite the process. She solved the problem simply—by buying an apartment in town—but the three of them spent almost all of their time out in the country: the real heart of the music that was Don's business.

When the three Vs talk about Daddy Don's business, their pride is palpable. Vicki explains that her father's label, Starday, helped newcomers hit it big. "My dad's niche was he discovered people. And so before a big RCA would sign him up, my dad would sign him up, then the big people would come."

Mama V isn't a gusher, but she borders on it now, talking about her late husband's success and inherent goodwill. "He helped artists start their own publishing. He was always helping people. He wasn't just making money off them, he was trying to make them independent."

"He had really good instinct," Vicki says, and then breaks into her wide grin. "I have to say, in high school—this is when the Beatles were hot and Elvis Presley—I was embarrassed that my father was in the country music business. I can remember even sort of hedging when people asked me what my dad did, and I would say, publishing, hoping that they would think religious pamphlets, or anything! And then my dad bought another label, in Cincinnati, "King," that had James Brown. And then I was proud for the world to know that my dad was a music publisher and he had James Brown!"

It wasn't necessarily in Don's blood to socialize with the stars, though he and Vadis did attend the big parties, looking the part of handsome executive and stylish wife. Because of Don's magnetic personality and kindness, though, he couldn't help but form lasting friendships with many of the artists he met along the way: Porter Wagoner, Conway Twitty, Jimmy Dean, Minnie Pearl, and Perry Como, to name a mere few.

The fact that Don not only worked but also lived among many of country music's biggest stars helped to secure these friendships. What he shared with Conway Twitty and Johnny Russell and just about all the members of The Oak Ridge Boys, plus a number of other singer/songwriters, was not only country music but a piece of the country itself, namely the farmland outside of Nashville in Sumner County. As Vicki explains, "Back then you could get a lot of acreage on the lake, so it was a place that evolved as a home to the stars." And the Pierce family was at the forefront of this evolution.

Don and Vadis made their entrance at a BMI party held at Belle Meade Country Club in the mid '60s.

As savvy as Don was in navigating the music industry, he always understood the inherent value in land. Growing up three blocks from a 100-acre park bounded by a lake and having rented his mother's cottage fronting Lake Washington in the early days of his marriage, Don had a particular understanding not only of the power of land, but of the power of land alongside a lake. In the short memoir he wrote for his family (upon their insistent prompting), Don recalls feeling that he had "died and gone to heaven" when moving to their first lakefront lot in Hendersonville, a home not far down the lake from Shawnee Waters. Recognizing its incredible value, he later used the proceeds he made by selling Starday to invest in more land in that area, an area that was increasingly known as a "home to the stars."

Shawnee Waters

The story of Shawnee Waters, the 33-acre peninsula on Old Hickory Lake where the Pierce family finally settled, is in many ways the story of country music, and not just because the money from the music went right into its grounds. The architect that Don and Vadis hired was Braxton Dixon, famous for designing the homes of many of those country music legends who were their neighbors but more importantly their friends.

"The house was Momma's creation, and she worked very closely with Braxton Dixon, who also built Johnny Cash's home," Vicki says.

Vadie asks her grandmother whose house was built first, theirs or the Cash's, and Mama V tells her that they were built almost together.

"They look so much alike," Vadie responds. "His was closer to the water. I remember when June died, we drove by the dock and there were all these flowers that people had brought and just put on their dock. And then Johnny died two months after June. My grandmother and grandfather went to Johnny and June's wedding, which was a tiny little wedding."

When asked what she remembers of it, Mama V's answer is sudden and sharp: "I remember that she wouldn't let anyone drink and they didn't have a bar. And everyone importuned me to go home and put a bar in the trunk of my car. I said 'I'm not gonna do that. This is her party.'" Mama V goes on to say that she flat out told those folks to go "find another sucker." Her attitude is due in part to a frankness that has, as usual, increased with age, but it is also due to her and Don's understanding of the depth of Johnny's struggle with alcohol. Having invited him to stay in their guest cottage during turbulent times, they both knew just how destructive his habit could be.

Framed on the wall in the living room is a relic of this friendship with Johnny Cash. On what appears to be a hide of some sort in deep red ink, which Johnny claimed was blood, is a humorous tribute to Don with a title

evocative of Huck and Tom. Johnny dubs Don, "A Feller I'd Like to Ride the River With," and honors him with a song about a dying man reflecting on the good he's done. Block capital letters written vertically along the side of the song read "copyrightable, cause was made up and meant by Johnny Cash Month of August YOOL 1966."

This treasured memento is at home in a house full of rare art and unusual finds, in a house that is itself a kind of rare art and unusual find. The Pierce's house, like the Cash's before it burned, is classic Dixon, which is to say it is reminiscent of Frank Lloyd Wright and incredibly innovative for its time. Built in 1969, the house features massive circular rather than rectangular spaces, with windows and balconies running the full length of the façade. The design was so architecturally striking that the house was later used as a movie set for what Vicki calls "a couple of really bad movies," including the 1979 thriller *Murder in Music City.*

The house took three years to build under Mama V's close supervision.

"His houses all have this great, Mediterranean feel would you say?" Vicki ventures.

"I think it's so California," her daughter chimes.

"It's so close to nature," Vicki comments. "His houses all nestle into the land they're built on."

Mama V herself doesn't elaborate much in the way of the house, though it is she who lives here full-time. Vadie visits from New York as often as her art career will allow; Vicki comes out frequently to work in the garden or tend to the trees and to bring her mother company. But it is Mama V who wakes up here every morning and who watches the sun ease into the lake every night. It is she who oversaw the house's design and decoration, juxtaposing the structure's modernity and coastal vibe with antique European finds, like the Venetian glass chandeliers that hang in the dining room and powder rooms. And though the house contains the collectibles she has bought on her travels, it very obviously holds her memories as well. Her late husband's room, for instance, she hasn't changed at all. His jackets and ties continue to hang in the closet.

"What's there is his," Mama V declares matter-of-factly. "The only thing I got rid of were his shoes," she says, then adds the after-thought: "I kept his boots."

"In fact, Vadie wore *his* boots to *his* funeral," Vicki adds. Wearing those cowboy boots was an uncon-ventional sign of respect that only Vadie, with her creative spirit and candid self-assurance, could effec-tively pull off. It was a tribute, though, that all three women could fully embrace and understand.

As much as Mama V misses her husband, her days are not spent sitting in Don's room or looking over old pictures. Instead, she keeps herself busy by cooking and reading, playing bridge and figuring out word games. She is eighty-five and healthy, proud that her doctor thinks she could pass for almost fifteen years younger.

"He says I could pass for 62. I think attitude has a lot to do with it. I'm an optimist," she says. "You laugh and the world laughs with you." She softens her voice. "You cry and you cry alone." Mama V pauses then reasserts herself, "I have a very good attitude. And I walk, you know."

Mama V is too cautious to walk alone, but she and Vicki walk together just about every day Vicki is out at Shawnee Waters. Their path, a grassy one about two miles long, loops around the peninsula-shaped property and takes them past all the major points of interest. It takes them by the creek and the tennis court and the dock. It takes them by the orchard where cherry, apple, plum, pear, and peach trees grow and by their tidy square garden where pumpkins, eggplant, asparagus, squash, and watermelons flourish. Vicki saves the seeds of the fruit she eats when traveling abroad and mails them home to plant. This is how she happens to have French watermelons in Tennessee.

At any given point along the walk, Vicki might pause to observe a turtle sunbathing or Mama V might stoop to pet the cat, a stray that took a liking to their garden and eventually to the women themselves. The cat makes it the full two miles, as does Mama V, her pole in hand. At certain points on the path, whether steep or bumpy, Vicki extends a hand to her mother—no words needed or exchanged. Then the two continue on, curving back around to rejoin the lake, walking single file along its tranquil banks toward home.

Vicki's Trees

Vicki often heads out to the country to spend time with her mother, but she has another reason, too, a newfound passion that has proved incredibly compelling.

"Since Mama V put the easement on the property, my mom has turned the entire thirty-three acres into a Level 3 arboretum." Vadie proudly explains.

"Vadie is absolutely right," Vicki says, taking the reins of the story with exuberance. "That was another thing that The Land Trust got me going on. When we were taking the initial tour of the property, the representative would say 'Oh, I love this persimmon tree. Oh, you have such great white oaks here. Oh, da da da da.' And for forty-five minutes she, like, waxed and waned on these trees. And I thought, my goodness, this is our own property, and we just sort of lumped them in a category of trees…So after Mama put the conservation easement on, I became very interested in rare, endangered trees. I have a book about trees native to the Southeast and it lists seven endangered, rare trees. I started on this quest to locate them."

Vicki's quest took her to a nursery in Missouri, which had the Wafer Ash. The Georgia Plume Tree she found in New Jersey. And the Franklin Tree ended up being nearby in McMinnville.

"A *major* scavenger hunt," Vadie says, one that involved both mother and daughter scouring Google and Craigslist. "I'm in Manhattan talking about discovering the Wafer Ash," she jokes.

"And the funny part is," Vicki chimes in, "after paying for shipping from New Jersey and Missouri, I am googling one of the rare trees I hadn't found yet, and it turns out there's a nursery in Fairview, Tennessee that had all of them. Nobody can appreciate that fact more than I!"

Vicki has planted all seven endangered trees and is also involved in a project to save the American Chestnut, which suffered a blight in the early 1900s that nearly decimated the population. Near the entrance to the driveway, she has planted row upon row of a new hybrid chestnut, scientifically engineered to withstand that blight, and she has begun nursing seedling chestnuts to give away.

Closing the gate on the white picket fence surrounding her and her mother's vegetable garden, Vicki heads inside for dinner.

As passionate as she is about helping save the American Chestnut, Vicki is most excited about the newest additions to her arboretum: a line of eleven seedlings encased in pastel plastic tubes. Looking like a high school biology experiment, these seedlings are in actuality descendants of some of the nation's most sacred and historic trees, which Vicki learned about through a book titled *America's Famous and Historic Trees*.

"When I heard the title, I was sold," she says emphatically. "I just loved looking at all these trees and reading about them and knowing that they were being loved and honored and respected. And then I got to the end, and it turns out"—here her tone increases in excitement—"the author collects seeds from some of these trees, grows them, and sells them mail order! So then I was like, oh what trees am I gonna pick? Which trees am I gonna pick?" By now, she sounds like a little girl let loose in a candy shop.

Vicki ended up choosing a wide assortment of trees, some for their visual appeal, most for their historic value. The first in the line is a cherry tree, not her first but one descended from the grove on the Capitol Mall near Thomas Jefferson's Memorial. The second is a species she had never before heard of called Eve's Necklace, and the third is a red maple descended from those that inspired Thoreau during his sojourn at Walden Pond. Next, she comes upon a sweetgum. "I have tons of sweetgum, but this is descended from a sweetgum in the front yard of Robert E. Lee. This is an elm tree," she says, pressing on. "It's called a survivor tree because it's descended from an elm tree that survived the Oklahoma City terrorist attack."

The list continues. A sycamore descended from seeds that went to the moon and back on Apollo 14. A bur oak that appears in Mark Twain's books. A southern magnolia descended from the one outside the White House. This particular one is special because Andrew Jackson planted it in memory of his late wife, Rachel, whom Vadie is related to through her dad's side of the family.

Nearing the end of the line, Vicki stops to finger the leaves sprouting from the top of one of her tubes, which is there to shelter out the light and force the plant to grow straight upward. "This one is a honey locust. It provided shade for Abraham Lincoln when he was giving the Gettysburg Address, and it has pretty flowers. Can you imagine how excited I was when I got to the last chapter and realized I could get my hands on these!" she exclaims, her joy as tangible as the trees themselves.

Vicki's tree choices reveal a great deal about her: her whimsical side and her profound side, her sense of history and her sense of occasion, her devotion to the South and to the country as a whole. It's a rare kind of collection by a rare kind of woman, one who chooses to be, in effect, a tree soldier, physically devoted to their protection and honor. What Vicki gains from this project, though, extends beyond the obvious pleasure and pride she derives from the work. She has effectively planted herself in this land by planting these trees, making a physical and emotional investment in the distant future of

The orange tubes around Vicki's seedlings serve as a hothouse in the winter and as a protective marker during the warmer months when caretakers are mowing.

the landscape. If the land is her father's legacy and the house her mother's, then the trees are indisputably Vicki's legacy, one that will continue to become more visible and more fruitful over time.

Queen Bee

What Vadie brings to Shawnee Waters is even less visible than her mother's seedlings are now, though it, too, will only become more fruitful over time.

In his memoir Daddy Don descibes Vadie as someone whose "good looks and talent are exceeded only by her charm" and though she would shrug off this compliment, she would do so with an enchanting smile because her grandfather is correct. Unlike her grandmother who describes herself as quiet and her grandfather whom Mama V describes as "basically a recluse," Vadie is magnetically social. She is the kind of person to give repeated hugs and to hold on to a person's elbows while she talks to them. She can hone in that way, look right into that person's face, nod at what they are saying, and thereby invite them into her space, her life, her home.

Though she grew up in a subdivision in Nashville and now lives in New York, often traveling the world to install exhibitions of her art, Vadie's home has always been very much at Shawnee Waters. It was the location of her first birthday party and of many subsequent ones. End-of-the-year parties for school were often celebrated around its pool. Slumber parties had friends sleeping on the floor of the playroom, and camping outings had those same friends in sleeping bags under the stars.

Shawnee Waters has always been Vadie's place for entertaining, and since Mama V remodeled one wing of the house to serve as Vadie's own studio and apartment, it has become even more so. She hosts camp reunions and bachelorette parties here. She throws Labor Day and Memorial Day celebrations, extending the use of the tennis court, the boat, and the pool to her friends and their children, building a bonfire for evening story-telling and smores-making. Vadie is always at the center of the crowd, bringing drinks, delighting children, leading the charge.

Over forty of Vadie's friends, including young children and their parents, gather for the annual Memorial Day festivities at Mama V's.

Vicki jokes about this, about Vadie's sociability in contrast to the family's relative shyness. "I think Vadie definitely got all the social genes. Wherever she could find them! Snag a few here, snag a few there!" she says with hearty laughter. "They all just sort of resonated in her."

Even so, Mama V and Vicki are hardly ones to miss the action. They are always present at Vadie's gatherings, participating in the fun that the third V conjures, enjoying the sense of vitality that she brings to the place. One of their favorite tricks—bringing guests to see the bees—is a show that actually features Vicki, even though the idea originated with Vadie.

"Vadie always wanted us to make our own honey, and this is one of the few things I had not been enthusiastic about," Vicki admits. She did know of an active hive in one of their sassafras trees near their tennis court, and when she noticed peculiar behavior in that hive one afternoon, she took it as "divine intervention!" and called on a friend who happened to be a beekeeper to help her. Vicki explains that when a queen bee detects she is running out of space in her hive, she lays a special "queen egg" then leaves with half of the force to find a new home. "He

As Vadie calms the bees with a tool called a bee smoker, Vicki—dressed in a full beekeeper suit—displays the latest harvest of honey.

said as long as I get the queen, the rest of them will follow me wherever I put the hive, so we started looking for a place to put it."

"It's interesting. The swarm takes on the queen's personality," Vadie says, then seeing her opportunity, adds, "It's fortunate we don't have a bitchy queen." She nails the joke, and all three women laugh together.

When they do their bee show, Vicki dons the full beekeeper attire and confidently approaches the white box with the word "Honeybees" Vadie painted on it in red. "The irony is, I'm all covered up to the nines, but all the people doing the observing are right there, half-naked, like Vadie in her swimming suit." Vadie did in fact get stung on one such occasion, but her exuberance for the honey-making has not waned.

It is a fitting interest for her because, as Vicki explains, when the queen bee leaves to find a new home, it is the daughter who becomes the new queen. She is the one left to preside over the original hive. The parallel is obvious: Vadie will one day move to Shawnee Waters and make it her own.

Tipping Point

This is a wish Daddy Don clearly expressed in his writings: "We dearly hope the time will come when Vadie will want to return to her home city of Nashville, Tennessee, and be with us in Nashville and Shawnee Waters."

Putting the property in The Land Trust was not necessarily Daddy Don's wish. In fact, all three women agree that he didn't even know about The Land Trust. But it is a decision that they all feel he would have embraced.

"It was really The Land Trust that was the beginning, the tipping point for us on this huge emotional investment in the property," Vadie says. "When I was a kid, you took it all for granted. You just end up here, and this is your house. No one is pinching you, saying this is a miracle. And Daddy Don *loved* this land. It's not that we didn't love it, but we didn't really, fully get it until after he died. Is that fair?"

"I think." Her mother pauses. "You're right."

The three women have put on warm clothes to walk their path. Vadie's red Navajo-style scarf matches Mama V's mittens. Vicki keeps her hands tucked in her back pockets. As they walk, they plan to collect fallen branches, branches that will be painted white and used as centerpieces, once dressed with the bright tissue-paper flowers they have spent so much time making. Before they set out, though, they visit the location where the wedding will be held and envision the day. Wreaths will hang from the sweetgum tree and quilts will be spread on the grass where guests can sit.

These three have shared the most sacred of moments here before. After Daddy Don's funeral, the three of them brought his ashes out to Shawnee Waters and, without discussing it at all, knew exactly what to do with them. Vadie handed her mother her journal as the three of them set out to walk the familiar path. In it, she had written a list of memorable moments from Daddy Don's life, which Vicki read aloud as they went along.

The young couple's initials—C.E. and V.T.—forever mark the tree stump where they will soon be married.

"We walked. And read. And laughed. And cried. And spread his ashes as we went," Vadie recalls softly. "In that private, little, incubated moment, it was perfect."

Looking out at the lake, thinking forward to her wedding and backward to her grandfather's passing, Vadie goes on: "It's not all about Daddy Don's passing, but when someone dies, it's this beautiful feeling of knowing you are doing the right thing, over and over again. Spreading the ashes. Putting it in The Land Trust. Making it an arboretum. That is such a gorgeous feeling that you don't anticipate when someone you love dies. We just keep feeding the property in ways that we never did before it was in the Trust."

The mother of the bride looks to the stump by the water's edge where her daughter will marry. Carved there is a simple red heart with the initials of the young couple. "We might not have a long history—several generations previous," she says, "but what we are making up for in lack of time is intensity of love and commitment."

Mama V nods, smiling.

The Knight Family

Miradiddle

Dewey Knight didn't flinch when Lucy, his wife of forty years, brought home six ducks on a whim. Nor did he get angry when those ducks bred and hatched sixty "baby ones." He was humored, though, when he came home one afternoon to discover Lucy attempting to corral the entire lot of escape artists back into their wire pen. As with everything in their marriage, doing so took a team effort.

"But it come a big rain," Dewey says, picking up the thread of the story in his distinctively unassuming and amused voice. "Just a gully washer, one day. And there's one of 'em that I thought had drown-ed. So I said, 'Gimme a paper sack, and I'll carry him away in the morning.' I just laid him beside my toolbox on my truck. When I got to the farm and started to throw it away, it was wigglin' around."

Lucy giggles.

"So that night, I come in and says, 'Here's your duck. I brought it back.'"

This time, it's Dewey who chuckles. "And we kept that thing fourteen years."

Dewey goes on to tell how they tried to release it, setting it free in a pond with other ducks, but it wouldn't go. "It'd come swimming back to us," he says matter-of-factly but with a trace of satisfaction. "The duck went to sleep one day," he continues, "and a hawk—we'd been seein' a hawk—well, he come down and pulled its head off. Killed it." Dewey's words are harsh but his tone is gentle. The story's ending is sad, but the way it's told—in Dewey's characteristically easy, straightforward manner—makes it only natural, as death usually is, and therefore okay.

Lucy is more apt to confide emotion, but she shares her husband's ability to cope: "That broke my heart when I went out there and found that duck. I heard the commotion, but I couldn't get there quick enough to help out or anything. I just—all I could do was pick her up and bring her in. She was already dead. She was a miracle from what happened, you know. So I called her Miradiddle."

This kind of narrative duet is characteristic of Dewey and Lucy Knight. Their story is ripe with loss—the loss of a daughter, the loss of a community, the loss of an era—but they view their past together squarely and with a softness, even a splash of humor, perhaps because they are still able to tell it together. Flipping through old pictures, recalling the history of their land and marriage, Dewey and Lucy's sentences have a habit of overlapping and interlocking. Any hardness melts. That's why the story of the Knights' property in Smith County is as much a love story as it is the story of a farm that has kept steady pace with time.

Where the River Bends

When Dewey Knight was born in 1926, he came into a corner of Tennessee where the Cumberland River arches to form a horseshoe in a protected enclave called The Bend. At that time, there was no hospital for the people living there, cut off as they were by the curving river and limited roadways. So the people had to summon the doctor using a shifty telephone, its wires prone to crossing in the wind, and wait for his arrival, often on horseback. Without a hospital, women in The Bend like Dewey's mother delivered their children at home and relied on the help of neighbors to clean up after the births and care for their newborns.

This was the kind of community where neighbors would even step in to help raise other families' children if the need arose. The Knights already had two children—a daughter, Wynema, and their son, Dewey, seven years younger—but as Dewey recalls, "There was a family living on The Bend that had a bunch of kids. Couldn't feed them, take care of them, really. The county wanted somebody to take some of them. So, my Mother and Daddy took a boy. He was nine-year-old at that time." Just like that, Dewey had

"At one time that many people lived on that farm," Dewey says of this picture taken in front of the Big House in 1933. Alongside the various tenant farmers and their families stand Dewey's parents, in the center behind Granny King, and Dewey as a little boy.

a brother, Ernest, who ended up staying on the farm until he was married with children of his own—about thirty years in Dewey's estimate.

Dewey's understanding of family has always extended outside blood relations in this way. His middle name, King, came from a woman who helped raise him but who had no biological connection to the family. "Granny King," as Dewey calls her, lived in "The Big House" with the Knights until 1934 when she, along with a number of other folks from The Bend, passed away in a particularly harsh winter. In photos, it is Granny King in her long black dress whom Dewey stands next to.

This inclusivity wasn't unique to the Knights: that's just how it was in The Bend. "It was a great community down that one section," Lucy explains. "All the people in there were very…" she pauses, looking for the right word. "…good. We used to have a lot of fun going to one another's home on the weekend and playin' cards, havin' chicken soup or barbeque rabbit." Here she chuckles, as she often does.

"Play Rook, " Dewey adds.

"Play Rook, you know," Lucy says, her words echoing her husband's effortlessly.

It was among this extended network of families from The Bend that Dewey made his friends and identified his boyhood heroes. Like his parents, who had to ford the river carrying their "Sunday shoes" and redress on the other side, Dewey and his buddies used to canoe across the river, then walk to Carthage to the "movie house," then walk back again, about six miles roundtrip. Seeing those Westerns expanded the boys' repertoire of games from Dominoes and Checkers to Outlaws and Indians. Emulating Roy Rogers, Dewey came up with stunts of his own, like standing upright on the broad side of a pony's back.

"Kids back then, they just made their own fun," he says.

"All the families just visited together," Lucy adds. "Course when the revival would be going on once a year, everybody would go home with somebody else for lunch that day. The men would get together and play ball. It was a sad time when the dam, *the dam,*" Lucy chuckles again, as if in nod to the homonym, "took all that up, broke the homes up. People moved out and scattered, you know."

The dam in reference is the Cordell Hull Dam, located at mile marker 313.5 of the Cumberland River. Construction began on the project in 1963, with its initial cost estimated at close to $80 million. The cost to the Knights, however, was more personal. They lost sixty-two acres of their land to the project, but more importantly, they lost their community.

"It got all the neighbors, aside from our family," Dewey says, explaining that the government bought five or six nearby farms in order to build the dam. "So we're all the farm that's left in here. The neighbors were just like family, you know. Back then, they were just like family," he repeats.

Topping Off

For most of the families in The Bend, including the Knights, farming was their work and their way of life, and for Dewey it still is. His parents bought the initial section of their farm in 1925 and the rest of it a few years later, with the total acreage now at 425. The Knight farm is considered to be one of the oldest in the county, having initially been part of North Carolina before the land became Tennessee territory.

Since toddlerhood, when he would perch on the tractor seat holding onto a steering wheel bigger than he was, Dewey has worked this historic farm. In the earliest years, he worked alongside his mother and his daddy, whom he remembers as a "big man, way over six foot." But at only seven-years-old, Dewey lost his father to an automobile accident, an accident that then left Dewey's mother responsible for running the place. Doing so required help, which came in the form of tenant farmers, locals mostly, who needed the work.

Dewey driving a load of tobacco in the 1950s.

As Dewey explains it: "There used to be four rent houses on this farm and they was always full. Cause there wasn't nowhere else for people to go; everybody made a livin' off the farm. There wadn't no government handout or nothing like that then… Some of em stayed five, six, seven years. Some of em just stayed one year then go to another farm. They was all from around Carthage, I guess, cause people didn't move a long ways off then like they do now, you know."

It was among these tenant farmers that Dewey learned to work the land, first by bringing water to the workers and gradually by handling the crops himself. "When they set tobacco, we'd haul water and stuff like that. Tote tobacco plants. Got big enough to drop em, then got big enough to set em out. And we thought we was doing good, but we was going the wrong way!" He laughs recalling these mistakes he made early in his farming career.

By age thirteen, Dewey was a member of the FFA (Future Farmers of America) and by seventeen, his senior year in high school, he was

attending class until noon, then coming home to work the fields until dark. "So, I've been farming ever since. They say you don't get rich off it but you can make a good livin' if you work it. And if you're happy doing it, well that's all that matters. That's the way I look at it."

Dewey's farming sense and his perseverance have enabled him to outlast the construction of the dam and the deterioration of local agriculture that followed. In his eight decades as a farmer, he has tried his hand at various profit-seeking ventures, including raising hogs, corn and tobacco crops, and more recently cattle.

"We didn't have many cattle back then and we raised a lot of hogs and put everything in corn and tobacco, you know, but when help got short, well I got out of the hog business and just went to cattle and raised tobacco. When it got to where I wadn't able to tend that—"

Every morning Dewey bottle-feeds his twin calves, supplementing their mother's milk.

Here Dewey stops. It's a sentence he can't finish because at 83, Dewey continues to come out and work the farm every day. Some things have changed. He no longer lives on the farm and hasn't since 1960, when he and Lucy moved closer to Carthage. He now drives a truck, following a "striped road with them two yellow lines" to get there. He has to use a four-wheeler to herd his cattle. But Dewey still handles the farm on his own, a fact he acknowledges with more frankness than pride.

"I hadn't had any help in twenty years except to pick up someone now and then. I cut my hay and rake it. I hadn't got a roller, so I hire somebody to roll it up but I do the rest…As far as somebody here every day, I hadn't had anybody in twenty-five, thirty years."

Except Lucy, who was his tractor driver.

"When we were younger, and I was helping on the farm, sometimes I'd ride the tractor from right after lunch until dark, all afternoon long driving to set tobacco," Lucy says. Here, she allows herself some nostalgia but grounds it, as she and her husband both tend to do, in basic human truth. "You know in those days, when we were havin' to do all those things, it was a chore more or less for him and for me, too. In other words, it was a job and you weren't crazy 'bout it but since then and we've got where we're not able to do it, now we say sometimes, 'It'd kind of be nice if we was able to do that again, wouldn't it.'" After a chuckle, she affirms, "That's how life is."

Dewey tells of working until 9:00 at night setting tobacco with his wife and tells of the year the black shank fungus took their crop. He tells of "toppin' off the hogs" to maximize their weight, of moving and rebuilding barns, of bottle-feeding numerous sets of twin calves. He marvels that at one point in time they actually picked acres of corn one ear at a time.

"I've spent my life here," he says. "That's all I've ever done is work on this farm. Somebody asked me if I didn't get lonesome out here, but I never have gotten lonesome out here." It would be hard to, for someone born to farm as Dewey was. The river makes a nice lunch spot. The trees are dependable company, as are the cows. The soil responds to his touch. The flowers console him.

Looking out at his property, he marvels not just at its history but also at its beauty. "If you can find a prettier place than this, well I'd love to see it," Dewey says, without waiting for an answer.

Looking out at his property,

he marvels not just at its

history but also at its beauty.

"If you can find a prettier place

than this, well I'd love to see it."

Home Fires

Dewey Knight and Lucy McCall got married in Ringgold, Georgia in June of 1947.

"Right across from the Chattanooga line," Dewey says, explaining that Ringgold was a town as close to Tennessee as possible but not in Tennessee, because, as he tells it, "You couldn't get married here without waiting three or four days, you know." They simply couldn't wait three or four days to get started on sixty-two years and counting.

Dewey visits the "Little House" where he and Lucy lived without electricity during their first winter together.

To prepare for their first winter together, Dewey and Lucy preserved 700 cans of meat, vegetables and fruits; at that time, the only goods they bought from the store were coffee and sugar. "We even killed hogs and canned pork," Lucy recalls. "Had to put the sausage in this kettle and cook it so long in that water bath. Although it was a job at that time, when you opened a can of that and warmed it, it was delicious."

"At one time there was two acre orchards on that place," Dewey adds. "And back then, you didn't have to spray em or nothin'. You just had plenty of fruit and nothin' bothered them, like they do now. We'd can 100 cans of blackberries. We miss that because you can't find no blackberries now hardly."

Their most vivid memories are of that first winter, when they had moved into the Little House on the other end of the farm from the Big House. At the time, the house had no electricity, only a "pot-bellied stove," as Lucy calls it. "I remember how cold it was. How hard it was to heat. We just had running water to the one faucet in the kitchen. We had a bathtub in the corner of a closet. You just warmed your water and poured it in that tub and you took a sponge bath, more or less, in the tub."

"In the living room, if you'd call it a living room, where we slept and everything, we had a fireplace in there," Dewey says. "The fires would go out, just like everybody else's, and we'd get up in the morning and there'd be ice in the kitchen in the water bucket!" He flashes his wife a smile. "It was back to the Daniel Boone days back then!"

The memories prompt Dewey and Lucy to tell about the time they hung their daughter's swing over the bed, so that she could bounce up where the air was warmer. "We had her where her feet could touch the bed, and she could kick around," Dewey tells while Lucy nods, both smiling.

This story reminds Dewey of another one, from his own childhood: "I went to visit my grandmother—tell you how the house was, it had an upstairs—I slept upstairs. The next morning it come a big snow. Of course we had a feather bed…All the cover we could sleep under but it snowed on the bed."

"It snowed on the bed," he repeats, laughing. "It blowed through the cracks. It sure did. I remember that well."

"He has told that many times," Lucy says. "Course that was before our time."

Their time didn't officially begin until 1945 when the two started dating, but they had been in the same grade at Carthage High School and in typing class together there. "We didn't even know one another existed really—till we got out of school," Dewey tells. "I got her to do some typing. She was better at that than I was…But we got out of school and it was at least two years before we ever started dating."

And not long after that before they were married. When it was time for Lucy to come to the farm where she and her husband would live, she had no idea how to get there on her own. "There's different roads to turn different ways off of that main road," Lucy explains. "He had tried to tell me, well, don't turn off any of these. But every time I'd pass one, I'd wonder if I'd done the right thing."

Dewey and Lucy cutting the "wedding cake" that Dewey's sister made after their honeymoon.

There is no mistake: Lucy did the right thing. She found home in Dewey. The two of them sit in their sunroom, hands resting one on top of the other in the exact way they did when cutting their wedding cake in the summer of '47. He can't help but brag about her, a warm smile on his face as he tells how she started playing the piano at age thirteen and how she has played every Sunday at church since then. It is clear: as much as Dewey loves the farm, it's Lucy who has his heart. And since her heart attack and bypass in 2007, his priority is now to care for her.

"He was always on the farm, always busy, never had any time to do anything in the house like cook or anything like that," Lucy says. "Course after I had my operation, he learned how to do laundry and cook and he

In the kitchen of their home near Carthage, Dewey and Lucy work together to finish the household chores.

gets up every morning and fixes our breakfast. And he had NEVER done any of that."

"You get hungry, you learn," Dewey responds, but he is joking. These days, he is up before 5, has the stove on at 5:30, and has their breakfast cooked by 6:00. He takes care of her, and she him. She makes bottles for the calves, and he empties the dishwasher, but the real thing of it is, they continue to giggle over one another, after over sixty years together.

Buttercups

The only other soft spot Dewey and Lucy have, besides the one each has for the other, becomes obvious in the rare pauses that arise when they tell their story. This happens when the subject shifts to their daughter. In these moments, their silence interweaves just as their words do. It's not a hard silence; rather, it's fleshy, warm.

Their only child, Loleta, was born in 1951, four years after her parents were married. They have a picture of her, taken when she was maybe two or three. In it, she is sitting on a wooden step, one shoe off, one shoe on, a straw hat behind her. She is holding a doll that resembles the dolls now decorating their sunroom some sixty years later. By the windows, Lucy and Dewey keep one particular doll in a crib, its cap on, its body tucked under a blanket, protected and safe.

The Knights have outlived Loleta, who passed away at age forty-seven of breast cancer. She had already married and made a life away from home, but a few years before her death, she decided to come back to the family farm. So Dewey put a doublewide trailer on the crest of a hill where Loleta and her husband could live and commute to work. Dewey recalls her saying that when she would drive away from town and return to the farm, she felt herself finally able to relax. She rests there now, near Granny King, in the little cemetery that dates back to 1859.

When their daughter died, Dewey promised Lucy that he would get the graveyard looking nicer: rebuild the fence, do some planting. Dewey mentions the "yellow flowers" but it is Lucy who elaborates: "At the time she was buried, there were no buttercups, maybe three or four scattered here and there. And now when spring comes, that's a solid mass." It's as if the land itself comes to honor the family's grave with flowers. In this spot, beside Loleta's grave, Dewey has also readied burial plots for the two of them.

The Knights made the decision to put their land in The Trust because they didn't want it to be split up. This destructive force, the erosion of beautiful pieces of property for development or government projects, is one this farm has contended with for decades. Reading about conservation easements in the local paper, Dewey knew that was what he wanted to do. He is conscious of the changes the farm has already undergone—bits chipped and added here and there, the advent of city water only seven years ago—and he is conscientious in planning how it will evolve further. He has picked out three sites for future houses, places where another family of the next generation might want to build and settle. "You just have to change with the time," he says simply.

Dewey is sensible in his preparations, but the vision of him going about them is romantic. Standing on the highest point of his property, looking out over the horseshoe of the river that forms The Bend, Dewey's figure in silhouette looks as rooted in the ground, as enduring and elemental and steadfast as the tree trunks that surround him. He will live on here, he and Lucy and their daughter Loleta, among the yellow flowers that bloom out year after year in the bend of the river.

The Ozburn Family

Bell Cow

"You know what a bell cow means, don't you?"

Fresh off his four-wheeler in sunglasses, a ball cap, and blue jeans, Perry Ozburn is hearty and down-to-earth, the kind of guy who's got you a cold drink before you can even get your coat off. But something in the way he stands, with his shoulders back and his fingertips wedged in his pockets, and something about the way he poses the question, authoritative even in its good-ole-boy accent, suggests that this is a man accustomed to being in charge. His question is clearly a rhetorical one.

"I used to tell my guys that worked for me," Perry says, referencing the family company, Ozburn-Hessey Logistics, where he worked for thirty-five years, twenty of them as the CEO. "Said, 'If you put two cows in a field, one will lead the other.' And people are the same way. So the bell cow—" he says, circling back. "You find the old cow that's gonna lead the whole herd…and you put the bell around that cow. And so when you call her, here she's comin', and those other ones will hear it and they'll follow in right behind her. And they'll come right to the barn. So that's why you call 'em the bell cow, 'cause they're the leader."

The analogy could not be any more fitting for the man using it. Professionally, Perry helped grow his father's business to become one of the top ten logistics companies in the world, now with an estimated 7000 employees globally. He also founded his own company in 1995, Ozburn Properties, LLC, and has since been successfully involved in commercial real estate and development deals. But Perry's capacity for leadership extends beyond business. It is in the work of family unity and continuity where he is perhaps most clearly a bell cow in his own right.

Over the past thirty-six years, Perry has taken ownership of nearly 500 contiguous acres of land in Williamson County, sections of which have been in his family for eight generations, dating back to 1804. He has revitalized it, restored several of its original buildings, organized its rich history, and ultimately secured it for future generations through his partnership with The Land Trust. Keeping the Ozburn stories and land intact is a crucial but only partial piece of Perry's more central commitment to the notion of family.

The story of Perry's own nuclear family is not perfect—divorced and remarried, he became a prominent figure in his oldest son's life only when the boy reached his late teens—but seeing him host a family get-together on a sunny weekend in April, all smiles as he gathers the generations for a hayride and a mess of hamburgers, Perry is clearly their unifying force and beloved patriarch. Old-fashioned in that he believes you can't be your kids' friend when they're young, he clearly shows that you can be their friend when they're older—and act as their mentor all along.

"I've led some people," Perry does acknowledge, modest grumble permitting. "I can't say that I'm, um, you know, none of us are ever what we'd like to be. But, I've had my share of success, and I'm very blessed and thankful for that."

Saying this, Perry is referring to his professional life, but it is a claim he can confidently make about his family life, too. In a culture where so many are unmoored from their ancestry and feel lost as a result of it, this is a guy who knows his roots and tends them. He teaches his kids and grandkids to do the same, sharing with them the dual importance of conserving as well as enjoying the land, of preserving the stories of the past as well as making memorable ones in the present. Perry's family

has a relationship with this piece of land that extends far back and looks far forward, but at the center is the sound of this man's bell, leading the others home.

Perry shares a laugh with his family after a day on the farm together.

Ozburn Hollow

Not one to dwell on himself—except to make a joke about his "wide part" or his well fed belly—Perry much prefers to talk about the farm instead. "Robert Ozburn, who came here somewhere between 1804 and 1806, he settled over this hill here," Perry says gesturing north-ward to the back of the property, though he could have pointed in almost any direc-tion as high wooded hills all but encircle this secluded strip of hollow.

"Robert, he served in the Revolutionary War about five different times. In the Revolutionary War," Perry elaborates, "you served three months and then you got out. I was reading up on him and like a lot of people in our family, he was contrary," Perry says, half-teasing, half-serious. "He wouldn't sign allegiance to the United States. He refused. He wouldn't have signed allegiance to anybody," Perry chuckles, taking obvious delight in this ancestor who made and lived by his own set of rules.

Perry goes on to explain that one of Robert's seven children, his son James, came over that same hill—called Chinkapin Hill for the old, gnarled oaks by that name which grow there—and purchased an adjacent tract of land, 170 acres on the banks of Arrington Creek, for $600. This was in 1831. James then chose a tucked-away site, in what came to be called

The 500-acre family farm encompasses an entire hollow that is just ten miles from downtown Franklin.

The farm's historic structures—built by Perry's great, great-grandfather—include the original home as well as a springhouse, smoke house, cellar and barn.

Ozburn Hollow, to build his home. It is this same hollow that Perry and his wife Elaine now own and the one they also call home.

Though he doesn't live in the old farmhouse that James built in 1834, Perry has invested considerable energy and time into refurbishing it. He has been careful to make the necessary repairs while maintaining the historic value, such as with reconstructing the stone-stack chimneys that had originally been secured using only mud and pig hair. He has also deconstructed and rebuilt the smokehouse "exactly like it was: same logs, same place, same everything" and has hung on its exterior many of the tools that his ancestors used throughout the centuries to work the land. It is a collection that holds a certain degree of magic for Perry.

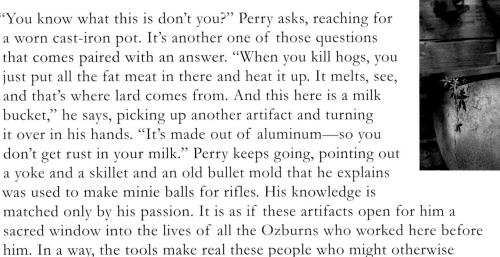

"You know what this is don't you?" Perry asks, reaching for a worn cast-iron pot. It's another one of those questions that comes paired with an answer. "When you kill hogs, you just put all the fat meat in there and heat it up. It melts, see, and that's where lard comes from. And this here is a milk bucket," he says, picking up another artifact and turning it over in his hands. "It's made out of aluminum—so you don't get rust in your milk." Perry keeps going, pointing out a yoke and a skillet and an old bullet mold that he explains was used to make minie balls for rifles. His knowledge is matched only by his passion. It is as if these artifacts open for him a sacred window into the lives of all the Ozburns who worked here before him. In a way, the tools make real these people who might otherwise merely be ghosts.

Over the Hill

One of Perry's favorite pictures is a portrait of the family taken in front of the old farmhouse, back in 1908 before the front porch was added. "This has all the family on it. That's my grandmother," he says, pointing to the purposeful woman on the left with both hands on her hips. "This is sister Willie—they called her Willie Dean. That's Pop there. That was my grandfather," he says, pointing to the man with the dark beard holding up a baby girl, whose name was Mildred but who was known to Perry as Aunt Mimi. Perry continues down the line pointing out the other people in

Perry's favorite picture, taken over one hundred years ago, shows his ancestors in front of the old farmhouse he has renovated.

the picture: his uncle J.B., Dessie, Ruth, Leslie, and the last person noted only as "Hired Man" whom Perry says "slept in the barn." But it is to Will, the older gentleman with the white beard, that he returns his attention. "That's Will; he was Pop's uncle. He gave Pop this house. It's an interesting story that tells you how they got the house," he begins.

The context for the story is the fact that the Ozburn farm was in the conflict zone during the Civil War, due in large part to the fact that one of the hills guarding the homestead is the highest point in Williamson County and readily accessible from only one direction. As such, it served as a signal tower during the war, a peak where soldiers used mirrors to relay intelligence from Franklin all the way to Murfreesboro. Perry reports that he and the men who help him maintain the farm find Civil War artifacts all the time, including two recently unearthed CSA belt buckles.

Fascinated by the richness of this Civil War history and adamant about preserving it, Perry hired a state archaeologist to come out and investigate, especially the old cemetery where Robert, the patriarch who died in 1834 at age 79, is buried. "There's eighty-two graves in there, and there's only thirty-two or three that are marked. The rest are just rocks. We think there's a lot of soldiers buried there because right across the hill over here was a hospital in the Civil War. There were 30,000 troops in this area, off and on during the war," Perry tells before getting back to the story of his great-great-uncle Will, who fought in the Civil War and who eventually gave Perry's grandfather the house.

The story goes that after suffering wounds to both his arms and his mouth, Will fell unconscious in the creek and awoke believing the water to be blood. Realizing he was all right, he walked over the hill back to his home, where he was greeted by his dog and family. He recovered and lived there, along with his mother, two sisters and brother, until they all died and left him alone and reportedly depressed.

William Wilson Ozburn once held title to the family homeplace.

One day his nephew, John Benton Smith Ozburn—Perry's grandfather—happened to walk over the hill and find his uncle sitting in the yard with tears streaming down his cheeks. Will invited John to bring his family to come live with him, promising him fifty acres of land including the house upon his death. True to his word, Will bequeathed John the house and land along with a few extra tokens of appreciation. As the third clause of his will reads: "I give and bequeathe to J.B. Ozburn and his wife Ellen my best bed and bed clothing thereon; also my watch as a family keepsake." And so it was that Perry's grandparents came to live in this storied house.

Distant View

His grandparents, John and Ellen, worked the farm and raised nine children before Ellen passed away in 1942 from—as Perry speculates—"just being worn out." Perry wasn't yet born when she died, but he does remember his grandfather "Pop" who lived on another fourteen years. Because Perry's father Frank was one of the youngest of the nine children, by the time Perry was a kid, Pop was very old, nearly ninety in Perry's memories of him.

Perry's grandfather, John Benton Ozburn, hunting on the farm.

"Around Pop, you made yourself scarce," Perry declares, "because if Pop saw you, he'd say, 'Go out there and pick me a basket of those tomatoes.' Or, 'Here, take my pocketknife and go cut us a mess a' okra,'" he tells, adopting a gruff, country accent for the impersonation. So he and his cousins, roughly twenty-five of them on the Ozburn side, learned to steer clear of chores by playing in the creek or climbing nearby trees.

Perry's mother, born Dorothy Smith Frey in 1914, also happened to be one of nine children. Like Frank, she had six sisters and two brothers: a coincidence that sparked immediate flirtation between the two when they first met. That flirtation led to a sixty-three year marriage—lasting until Frank's death in 2003—and four children, the oldest of whom is Perry.

It is early summer and Perry has brought his mother—who at ninety-six is as sharp and gracious as ever—to his house for a late morning visit. Though she probably could drive, he prefers to escort her and she lets him. Unlike Frank who had brown eyes and even browner hair—the distinctively handsome Ozburn look—Dorothy has arresting turquoise eyes, "killer eyes," Perry calls them as the two sit beneath the gently

whirling fans of
Perry's porch, talking
about the old days.

"Daddy always wanted
a little more land,"
Perry says, "and some
water and—"

"Cows," Dorothy
interposes gaily. "And
I wanted a house on
a hill with a creek, so
that's what we had,"
she says, smiling at the
memory of those early
years. Dorothy had
grown up three-to-a-
bed in Coopertown,

Tennessee, and eventually left home with eight dollars to her name before
making her way into nursing school. She always loved the outdoors,
though, so for she and Frank to have enough money to buy a thirty-acre
farm on Murray Lane, which at the time was just a single-lane gravel road,
was heaven to her. And to their four kids, who could therefore grow up
free to roam.

"They could go out, and I didn't know where they were for no tellin' how
long," Dorothy says, recalling how her sons especially would always be off
somewhere, filling their days with fishing and hunting, riding bareback and
"getting into the neighbors' ponds."

"And getting shot at," Perry adds teasingly, as they both laugh. "It was a
great childhood," he notes more seriously.

His "great childhood" was in some ways like his father's. Perry tells the
story of his dad and his Aunt Nell as young kids trapping raccoons and
skunks and opossums and selling the pelts so that Frank could buy a
single barrel shotgun that he wanted, a gun that Perry still has. Dorothy
tells matching stories of Perry catching frogs and bringing them home in

a paper sack only to have them get loose and hop all over the kitchen. She also recalls how they used to lie out in the yard together, finding animal shapes in the clouds. "That was fun to do," she reflects. "Nothing like growing up on a—a space. You know we had space, and we really enjoyed that."

"Yea, I gotta have my space," Perry echoes, as he watches the butterflies dapple the yard, following their flight up. "That is a Claude Monet sky there, Momma," he says unexpectedly, wistfully.

"Oh isn't that pretty," she says back in a mild voice, sweet and true.

"You can see the ridge all the way out there today. That's about ten miles probably. Could be twenty miles. It's a pretty good distance," Perry says, looking out, speaking softly the way people do when a beautiful view casts its singular kind of spell.

The view is the same one Perry's grandfather looked upon fondly in his day. "My grandfather used to say, 'You know when you're sittin' here and somebody's comin' up that road, they're comin' to see you.'" Perry pauses then adds by way of explanation, "It was a gravel driveway, so you could see the dust comin' up all the way out to where it hits the road." Perry smiles. It's a perfect little seam in the world right here, and like his ancestors before him, Perry knows it.

Here We Go

Perry and his wife Elaine had the idea to move here to the Ozburn farm in 1976, when they were one year married and looking for a place with the kind of "space" Perry had grown to cherish. At the time, his aunt Mimi— the one who was the baby girl in the old family photo—was still living in the old farmhouse, so Perry approached his father about buying a small parcel of the property where he and Elaine might build. As things went: "My dad came out and just told Mimi, said you know, let's keep this in the family." He offered her a deal that would enable him to buy the farm but would allow her to remain there and be financially looked after until her passing. "She said ok, she gave it to him, and then he gave it to us."

The gift from Frank to his newlywed son and daughter-in-law was 240 acres. (He also gave 260 acres to Perry's brother Marty, a share that Marty eventually sold to Perry, which accounts for the 500 contiguous acres he now owns.) When Perry and Elaine were given the land, though, it hadn't been worked in forty years so it was "all grown up, and there were big huge gullies coming down—bushes, scrubby trees everywhere." But this was just the kind of work that Perry liked. And Elaine, too.

"Elaine is not what I would call a domestic person," Perry says, cutting her a glance then laughing. "She can be as girly as any girl but she's not a—"

"I'm a tomboy," Elaine pipes in. Petite and youthful looking with brown shoulder-length hair and big blue eyes, Elaine exudes energy and a cheerful readiness to go and do. This, Perry acknowledges, is one of the things that caught his attention. "She doesn't like sitting at home, like *Leave it to Beaver* or something…That was one of the things that attracted me to her. She was so independent first of all and second of all she just enjoys the things that I enjoy." One of those things is clearly the outdoors. Another is work.

"Farm work was my release," Perry states. "I like to do that kind of stuff. So I brought a tractor and a bush hog out here and started cutting."

"And I did all the mowing," Elaine adds. "I wore out one John Deere," she says, with a clear measure of can-do and sass to her.

"The best memories we have, Elaine and I, was when we first moved out here because the place needed so much work. And we enjoyed doin' it."

In the midst of revitalizing the farm and building their new home, Perry and Elaine had their first child, Kit, in 1977.

Their plan was to have one more and be finished. "And then it just didn't happen," Perry explains, "so we went eleven years until finally—" Perry breaks off, the joy and the relief still with him even now. Finally, in 1988, their second son Ben was born when Perry was forty-three.

Though Kit and Ben were the ones raised on this farm, it is Chipper—Perry's oldest son from his previous marriage—who now lives here with his family. Chipper was raised in Chattanooga by his mother and stepfather, and though he was never officially adopted, they decided when he was very young to change his last name to Farley. Perry came to visit him early on, but, as Chipper explains, there was a stretch where the two didn't see each other very often. "It was just—it was complicated," Chipper says. "Nobody did anything wrong or anything like that. It was just, I was young. I didn't really understand what was going on."

The turning point in Chipper's relationship with Perry, as he calls his dad, happened when Chipper was in college. He arrived at school only to discover that his tuition hadn't been paid and that his stepfather no longer had the means to pay it. "There I was. And so, I called Perry. I think this is a real statement about his character. You know I hadn't talked to him in quite some time, years at this point, and I called him and said, 'You know I'm kind of in trouble down here.' And he got on a plane and flew down there the very next day. He just took care of it," Chipper says. "I mean, no questions or concerns. It was like, 'You need some help, I'll help ya. Here we go.' And that got it all going again; I was nineteen at that point."

Soon thereafter, Chipper came to Nashville to intern at the family company and met his fifteen-year-old brother, Kit, and his baby brother, Ben, for the first time. "Kit's a great guy. We hit it right off. We have a lot of things in common and it was really pretty easy. And Ben was a little kid at that point so that relationship was different…Ben has known me most of his life. But we all have great relationships. It's all been really pretty easy."

It's a remarkable, simple story of reconciliation. And a genuine one. When the family gathers for a day together in early spring, the ease that Chipper claims is evident, as is the mutual affection.

Pray-a-lot Hill

"Have we come to the right place?" Kit asks, stepping out of his car. He has dark hair like his mother and a smile like his father, but he is more soft-spoken than either of the two, even when he's joking.

"Yippee ki-yay. Oh look at those boots would ya!" Elaine exclaims, cheerfully greeting her grandchildren Carter, age six, and Anna Brooks, age three.

After the half-hour drive from Nashville out to the farm, Kit hops on the four-wheeler with his daughter Anna Brooks, as his son Carter joyfully races them.

Perry and Elaine aren't shy about saying who is the "loud family" and who is the "quiet family," who is country and who is citified, when it comes to their kids. When Kit's wife, Natalie, climbs out of the car, she is given an immediate dose of good-natured teasing about her shoes: a pair of pink rubber flats that Perry says is "as close to farmin' as Natalie gets." They clearly pin her crew as the citified side of the family.

Hugging Natalie and grinning, Perry launches into the story of "Pray-a-lot Hill," an obvious family favorite whose punch line has given lasting name to the hill that once served as the signal tower during the Civil War.

After some debate about when exactly the story took place, Perry sets the scene that Natalie, most likely age eighteen or nineteen, had come out for her first visit to the farm. "She was tryin' to not be scared of snakes or bugs or dirt or—" Perry pauses for effect then adds, "me!" as they all laugh boisterously. Perry decided the best way to show her the farm was to take her to the top for a bird's eye view, so they climbed into one of Perry's various farm vehicles and up they went.

"It's very steep," Natalie insists politely.

"It's really, really steep," Perry confirms. "So we went up the hill. That thing makes a lot of noise anyway, and it's in four-wheel drive," he says, adding a grumbling engine sound to enhance the drama. "When we got to the top, I said, 'Natalie what do you think of all this?'" In a tiny, scared voice, he imitates her infamous answer: "'Um, I just prayed a lot!'" Everybody bursts into laughter, Natalie included.

Perry starts to tell another story about feeding Natalie a piece of Christmas ham that had fallen on the floor when a voice from around the barn calls out, "Hey guys! I saw some four-wheelin' happenin' out here." It is Chipper, followed by his wife Dana, a smiling redhead whom Perry describes as a "what-you-see-is-what-you-get type person," a kindred spirit whom he adores. With them are their three kids—James, Lindsey and Lydia Farley—who hit the scene with unbridled enthusiasm. All of a sudden there is a burst of festive commotion as the families greet one another, the dads tossing kids in the air then exchanging baseball scores, the women talking dinner details and shoes, the kids debating about who will sit where on the hay wagon.

As the hayride begins, Dana and her daughters Lydia and Lindsey sit in front, while Elaine and the rest of the family fill in the back.

"Here's what we're gonna do," Perry announces to the group, corralling them to attention. "We're going up Pray-a-lot Hill, Natalie. We're gonna go up the fence row, round the corner, all the way around the top, then come down the valley."

"Oh, I love it up there. It's a good spot," Ben says. Ben has taken his place on the four- wheeler where he will bring up the rear. A senior at the University of Tennessee, Ben is a lot like his dad: quick-witted, good-natured, charming, confident. Though Chipper already lives on the farm, he and Perry both foresee that Ben will one day settle there, too, and help oversee it. It's a prediction Ben doesn't correct. "I love coming home," he says animatedly. "I live in downtown Knoxville and it's just so peaceful out here. I started working here when I was thirteen, lived here my whole life so…" he says trailing off, letting implication speak for itself.

Perry signals to Ben to ensure he is ready, then fires up the tractor and shifts into gear. Lurching forward, all the kids cry out "Adios, amigos!!" as they start across the pasture, heading toward Pray-a-lot Hill.

At various points along the climb, Perry cuts the engine to share a point of interest, the first being an old washtub where his father used to bring his mother when they were dating, another being the remnants of the earthworks the soldiers built and a spot called "Jeff's Cave," where a slave by that name supposedly lived during the war.

Approaching the last bit of incline, the heretofore-jovial hayride begins to sound more like a high-adrenaline roller coaster. Bouncing into one another, clawing for a stronghold, everybody whoops and squeals as they brace for the deep ruts and the steep angle up. Pretty soon, though, they grind to a halt and after much revving and little moving, it's clear that they are stuck. Perry calls for everybody off, and the wagon jerks its way to the top with the family members climbing after it.

At the top of the hill, Perry stops and waits, giving everyone else time to reach him.

"This right here is kind of a inspiration point for me," Perry tells them, once they have gathered around him. "Whenever I was being troubled by my children—"

"Now that never happened," Chipper answers in a slow, teasing way.

"Or having trouble with business or anything," Perry continues, not rising to the bait. "You know just when my dad died and stuff, I'd come up here.

And you can just sit here with the peace and quiet, and I mean it just, it works. You sit here 'til you're cleansed, and you're good to go back. Some things take longer than others," he adds, now cutting his eyes teasingly at his oldest son.

Further along, Perry stops again, letting the kids hop off and run around a little bit. He also gets down and then walks up through the woods to another one of his sacred spots. "This place right here in the fall—all of these are maples—it's the most spectacular place you have ever seen. When the sunlight's coming through the trees, it's just spectacular," he reiterates. "If you don't have faith, you can't come up here and believe in nothing," he says poignantly.

It's a fitting comment for a place nicknamed "Pray-a-lot Hill," but Perry doesn't pause for any more musings. He simply strides back to his tractor seat and calls the stragglers to come on: this ride isn't over yet. Apologizing for the bumpy climb, Perry makes a simple suggestion that sends the kids into a frenzy of excitement and the parents into a series of amused eye rolls. It's an invitation to play in the creek.

"Now that was a hard sell," Elaine jokes as the kids plunge down the banks toward the creek, the Farleys leading the way. In no time all five kids are in the water, splashing and throwing rocks and squealing.

"Ah, mom, these aren't waterproof!" James proclaims, lifting his boots to dump out the water gathered there.

"Well the reason is, James, the water's over the top of them," Perry tells his grandson.

"My undies are wet," Lindsey announces, not at all self-conscious. "Does anyone have an extra pair?"

"I got a pair; they might be a little big though," Perry answers, eyes twinkling.

Still in the creek, holding the hem of her skirt and trudging along in her boots, Lydia looks up and announces with a child's perfect blend of succinctness and hyperbole: "This is the best day of my life." Perry's only answer is a wide, wide smile.

Listen to the Music

Growing up out in the country, James, Lindsey and Lydia—ages ten, eight and five—are used to swinging on vines and hiking in the woods, playing in the mud and feeding chickens. They live just down the driveway from their grandparents in a log house that their great-uncle, Perry's brother Marty, built and later sold to Perry. Perry then gave the house along with five acres to Chipper and Dana, who moved there in 2001 when Dana was five-months pregnant. They have lived there ever since, and though it fluctuates, they currently share the residence with twenty animals, including four dogs, three cats, nine chickens, two birds, and two turtles—the turtles being only temporary pets that they bring home at the start of summer then re-release in the fall.

"When you grow up around the farm, the kids can go out and play," Dana says, "and she loves the chickens," she adds, nodding at Lindsey who was at one time all girly princess but who is now pure tomboy. Perry pays her to gather worms—ten cents a pop—for when they go fishing, and she has become the family's "little entrepreneur," gathering and selling eggs for two dollars a dozen.

"It's different, you know…Every night you come in to take a bath and you have to check yourself for ticks and it's just a way of life," Dana asserts.

"Do you remember when we were sittin' out on the front porch?" she says, turning to her youngest daughter, Lydia. "Do you remember what you said? The trees were rustlin'…the wind blowin'. You could hear the geese going honk, honk."

"It was beautiful," Lydia answers, taking herself back to that moment.

"It was," Dana says, hugging her close. "And you were like, 'Listen to the music, Mom. Listen to the music.'"

Living on the farm affords them mornings of listening to this rare kind of music. It also affords Chipper the opportunity to be outdoors hiking and biking the trails Perry has cut. It gives Dana, who calls herself "a

Lindsey, age eight, wants to earn enough money to buy a horse, so she tends to her family's eight chickens, selling their eggs for profit.

good country girl as long as I don't have to deal with the mice or the snakes," the chance to garden. And it gives the kids an entirely different childhood, one that fosters the same kind of independence that their uncles and grandfather and great-grandparents gained from growing up in the country. It's not without its challenges, Dana acknowledges, like she wishes there were a grocery store closer, but the benefits far outweigh the inconveniences.

One thing it has fostered for her kids is a sense of inclusion and togetherness. Without neighborhood kids to complicate the dynamic, they all play together, including Alex, Dana's nephew whom she and Chipper adopted four years ago. Dana had always been close to her sister's son, and through the years she witnessed the difficulty her sister experienced trying to be a single mother.

Alex, a rising senior in high school, proudly watches five-year-old Lydia run the bases on their pretend baseball diamond.

"Let's just say it was easier for us to do it than it was for her at that time," Chipper explains modestly. It is yet another example of the remarkable commitment to family, especially to extended family, that the Ozburns have been happy to make over the centuries.

Again, the choice hasn't been without its challenges, but it too clearly has its rewards. All the kids, especially James, look up to Alex who plays basketball and baseball with them, teaching them how to hold the bat and how to shoot lay-ups.

"Just the other day, Lindsey did something and got in trouble, and sweet Alex comes and picks her up right here and carries her upstairs. He is so sweet with them," Dana reflects then adds, "He looks up to Chipper. Him and Chipper have a good relationship, too. Chipper's like a big baby or a big kid—he loves to play." But he also clearly understands how to be a father, even to a teenage boy he hasn't previously raised. It's a role similar in some ways to the one Perry undertook with him when he wasn't much older—a fatherhood based solidly on integrity and love.

Dana recognizes a lot of similarities between Chipper and Perry—their love of sports, their love of the outdoors, and their love and concern for this particular piece of land. Chipper dreams of someday making it into a working farm based on a permaculture model he has recently learned about, where a farmer raises cows, hogs, and chickens, allowing them to graze systematically over a large portion of land, and then offers local clients installments of meat in a kind of "buying club."

"Looking far out into the future, once Perry's gone and all that, we'll need to come up with some kind of way I think to probably—" he doesn't quite finish his train of thought, but he is clearly thinking about how to maintain the farm once its chief steward has passed on. He is also keenly aware of the value of a piece of land like this one, now, in a time of economic uncertainty.

Easy-going by nature, Dana and Chipper are nevertheless very conscientious when it comes to deciding how to raise their four children.

"When the economy collapses, I'll have my chickens," he says sarcastically. "That's my running joke—'when the economy collapses….'" Joking aside, he continues his train of thought more solemnly: "I worry about my kids' genera-tion. I think we're going to get poorer as a country. That's another thing I'm so thankful for with this farm, this property. There's deer. And turkey. Not to sound like the Unabomber or something living out in the woods, but you know, if times get tough, you can live off the land to a degree."

For now, though, the Farleys are content simply to enjoy the land with its deer and its turkey, not to mention its proximity to Perry and Elaine.

Family Dinner

Gathering at Perry and Elaine's pool house—the hayride over, wet socks removed—Ben is obligingly tossing the football with James and Lindsey; Lydia, Anna Brooks and Carter are looking for the cat; the parents are sipping cold beers; and Perry is lighting the grill.

"He's a great griller," Natalie says earnestly. "Everything he makes is so good."

"Not really," answers Perry, "but I have cooked a few things. I will say this, when we were in our younger days, when we weren't conscious of our health, I could put some ribs out of here."

Chipper agrees, testifying that they tasted like "butter on a stick." But tonight, it's good old cheeseburgers. "I'm cooking these shorter than normal," Perry says. "My attention span is real short—"

"Like a goldfish," Ben quips before imploring James to "go long" for a pass, thus buying himself a few sips of his beer.

The guys are hanging out around the grill, talking politics and telling stories, one in particular about an "epic wreck" on a four-wheeler one night that landed Perry in the hospital with a separated shoulder. As the story goes, he quickly rejoined the party once home from the emergency room.

"I always like stories where I'm the butt of the joke," Perry laughs.

Ben tells stories of campouts on the farm with his fraternity brothers, and they all recall hosting Kit's bachelor party here and later his and Natalie's rehearsal dinner when the two married their junior year in college.

"Natalie—love her to death—she feeds their family perfectly," Perry says. "They don't eat any fat, everything's organic, bla, bla, bla. But Kit grew up eating my food on the grill. So today he'll get into these burgers…You know, I look at what my mother and father grew up on," he continues. "I think we lose the fact of—see my parents grew up with food that was all raised right there. My dad grew up in that house for eighteen years, he didn't eat much of anything that wasn't within sight."

"I have bacon, hot sauce and jalapenos, boys," Perry tells his sons. "Yes, yes, and yes," Chipper responds, as Ben adds with a smile, "I do like to come home."

It's a reminder of just how much the world has changed in one generation, much less the eight generations that have lived on this Dual Century farm. Sitting down to dinner, the Ozburns are in many ways a modern family. The talk around the table is all about *American Idol* and Facebook. Everybody's in jeans.

But in many ways, it is timeless. They are a family sharing a meal and stories and laughter—adults at one table, kids at another. They say grace. They talk over one another, agreeing and disagreeing. They eat too much and praise the chef. They hug goodnight.

"I always give thanks about my family," Perry says, referring to the kids and grandkids surrounding him but also to his parents, his siblings, and his cousins. "There's nothing worse than family members that don't speak to each other."

This is why, when Perry was initially trying to arrange his estate, he insisted on finding a way to "make sure the next generation can have it and not create any family problems. That's what I didn't want," he emphasizes. After considering turning the land into a public park, Perry learned about The Land Trust for Tennessee and knew that he had found his answer. It is one he feels his whole family has supported, and the fact that his cousin "just over the hill" has followed suit gives him just cause to think so.

As for his children, Chipper articulates what he believes all three sons feel: "I'm really glad he did it. I know Ben is, too. And Kit I'm sure feels the same way…Putting it in The Land Trust will keep it the way it is now, which is important to him. It's important to me, too. I would never want it to change from the way it is out here. But it also eliminates any potential debate over what should happen with the property. And," he adds, "it's certainly nice to see something that's going to persist and not get subdivided up into, you know, cranked-out spec houses."

"I'm a developer," Perry readily volunteers, "but I didn't want four houses per acre. There's nothing wrong with that if that's what people want— I just didn't want it here. There's just too much sweat that's been put in these hills."

Perry and Elaine have other houses in other places—a brownstone in downtown Franklin, a lake house on Tims Ford, a place in Florida. "We've got some good houses," he admits, "But when I think of home, this is where I think. This is always home to me."

Surrounded by his wife of thirty-five years, his three grown sons, his daughters-in-law, and his grandkids, surrounded by the presence of all the Ozburns who lived on the land before him and all those to follow, Perry's message is in fact much broader and more lasting. It is the message promised in any place—any farm or hill or field or hollow—that has been saved in perpetuity. That land, though owned by one person or one family, is really shared by everyone when it is preserved. Now and always, it becomes not just "home to me," but "home to us."

Honor Roll of Land Trust Partners

Between December 1999 and July 2012, The Land Trust for Tennessee signed conservation agreements with—or received gifts of land outright from—more than 200 parties; these cover an aggregate of almost 75,000 acres spread over roughly half of Tennessee's 95 counties, and range in size from less than a half-acre to more than 4,000 acres. The vast majority of these tracts are privately owned; about fifteen are held by government agencies or independent non-profit organizations. The parcels are listed here in the order in which the legal accords were completed. The names of the parties of record (or, in a few cases, an anonymous designation) are listed first, followed by the county in which each tract is located and the month/year of each agreement.

Aubrey Preston, Williamson County, December 1999
Cora Preston, Williamson County, February 2000
Denmark Bell, Williamson County, December 2000
Tom Beasley, Smith County, December 2000
Preston Ingram, Williamson County, December 2000
Lou Osburn Benson, Williamson County, June 2001
Agnes Womack, Williamson County, June 2001
Mary Ann and John Sugg, Williamson County, November 2001
Raymond and Linda White, Williamson County, December 2001
Aubrey Preston, Williamson County December 2001
Nathan Harsh, Sumner County, December 2001
Elizabeth Crunk, Williamson County, December 2001
Steve and Susan Fisher, Williamson County, July 2002
John Ingram, Williamson County, December 2002
Orrin Ingram, Williamson County, December 2002
Bill and Shirley McEwen, Hickman County, December 2002
Robert Lipman, Williamson County, December 2002
Nadie and George Ladd, Maury County, December 2002

Nadie and Thomas Gary Ladd, Maury County, December 2002

William Hostettler, Patrick Donlon, J.V. Crockett III, Hickman County,
    October 2003

The Holland Family, Carroll County, December 2003

Oak Grove Partnership, Hardeman/Fayette Counties, December 2003

Monette Anthony LLC, Grundy County, December 2003

Preston Ingram, Williamson County, December 2003

South Cumberland Regional Land Trust, Franklin County, April 2004

Roper's Knob, Heritage Foundation of Franklin and Williamson County,
    June 2004

John Rutledge, Humphreys/Hickman/Dickson Counties, December 2004

William and Eugenia Cammack, Hickman County, December 2004

Robbie Hassler, Pickett County, January 2005

Ora Thompson, Maury County, July 2005

Partners in Conservation, LLC, Hickman County, August 2005

James Earl and Cheri Cruze, Knox County, October 2005

Perry and Elaine Ozburn, Williamson County, December 2005

Ridley and Irene Wills, Williamson County, December 2005

Cecil D. Branstetter, Sr., Davidson County, December 2005

Cumberland Heights Foundation, Davidson County, June 2006

John and Gerrie Porter, Maury County, August 2006

Susan West, Davidson County, November 2006

Eslick and Annie Daniel, Maury County, December 2006

Bill and Walter Nunnelly, Hickman County, December 2006

Jane Merryman and Pam Newby, Sumner County, December 2006

Jay and Marcia Franks, Williamson County, December 2006

H.J. Moser (Mossy Creek Farms, LLC), Jefferson County, December 2006

David and Kathryn Gooch, Meigs County, December 2006

Greg Vital, Hamilton County, December 2006

Shelby Farms Park, Shelby County Government, February 2007

Stone Hall, Metro Government of Nashville and Davidson County,
    February 2007

Margaret Olson, Anderson County, March 2007

Nashville Commons LP, Davidson County, March 2007

Jessie Wells Baker, Pickett County, April 2007

Karen L. Guy, Davidson County, April 2007

Thomas Beasley, Smith County, April 2007

Collins Farm, Save the Franklin Battlefield Inc., Williamson County, July 2007

Nancy L. Adgent, Marshall County, July 2007

Harlinsdale Farm, City of Franklin, Williamson County, October 2007

Charles Mann, Maury County, October 2007

Ron and Marilyn Truex, Williamson County, November 2007

Travis and Katherine Robeson, Giles County, November 2007

Gerald and Genette Robeson, Giles County, November 2007

Alice Hooker, Giles/Marshall Counties, November 2007

Tennessee Tree Toppers, Sequatchie County, December 2007

Steve and Susan Bass, Maury County, December 2007

Corner Partners LLC, Davidson County, December 2007

Bill and Alice Fitts and family, Maury County, December 2007

Faith A. Young, Smith/ Trousdale Counties, December 2007

Leon and Cynthia Heron, Williamson County, December 2007

Allen Shoffner, Bedford County, December 2007

Mary Ann and John Sugg, Williamson County, December 2007

David and Elaine Alderson, Maury County, December 2007

Jack and Linda Vannatta, Bedford County, December 2007

David and Vivian Garrett, Williamson County, December 2007

Mike and Peggy Widener, Giles County, December 2007

Manuel and Janice Zeitlin, Perry County, December 2007

Alfred and Carney Farris, Robertson County, December 2007

Vadis L. Pierce, Sumner County, December 2007

Mack and Anne Finley, Robertson County, December 2007

Nell Wilson, Cheatham County, December 2007

Calvin and Marilyn Lehew, Williamson County, December 2007

Anne Sanders, Williamson County, December 2007

The Duncan Family, Perry County, December 2007

Rolland and Andrea Luplow, Dickson County, December 2007

Mike and Cindy Corn, Williamson County, December 2007
Emily Magid, Williamson County, December 2007
Brenda Bass, Williamson County, December 2007
Kerry Riley (Grundy Co., LLC), Grundy, December 2007
Anonymous, Hamilton County, December 2007
Franklin and Tamatha Farrow, Hamilton County, December 2007
The Mayfield Family, McMinn County, December 2007
Larry and Mary Evelyn Musick, Jefferson County, December 2007
Anonymous, Hamilton County, December 2007
Phillip and Mary Fortune, Greene County, December 2007
John P. Adams, Franklin County, December 2007
Lee Stapleton, Franklin County, December 2007
Warner and Madge Bass, Lewis County, December 2007
Hill and Emily McAlister, Giles County, December 2007
Mildred Stahlman, Humphreys County, December 2007
Mildred Stahlman, Williamson County, December 2007
Ricky Volner, Perry County, December 2007
Sumter Camp and Sherry Knott, Davidson County, December 2007
John Goodson (Meyers Point LLC), Franklin County, December 2007
Lost and Champion Coves, University of the South, Franklin County,
    February 2008
Dewey and Lucy Knight, Smith County, September 2008
Lee and Nancy Fleisher, Hickman County, September 2008
Harold Webb, Polk County, October 2008
Bowie Park, City of Fairview, Williamson County, October 2008
Howell Family Partnership, Montgomery County, November 2008
Bonita and David Barger, Putnam County, December 2008
Wayne Neese, Marshall County, December 2008
Zollie and Jenette McCormack, Giles County, December 2008
Jim and Dava Merritt, Franklin County, December 2008
John and Mary Cribbs, Giles County, December 2008
David and Jan Darden, Polk County, December 2008
Bill Brock, Bradley County, December 2008

Dan Walling, Van Buren County, December 2008

George and Ruby Dixson, Marion County, December 2008

Catherine Colby, Hamilton County, January 2009

Felicia Sells, Franklin County, March 2009

William Spann and Rolland and Andrea Luplow, Dickson County, June 2009

Phyllis S. Brock, McMinn County, July 2009

Kurt Johnson (Paynes Cove LLC), Grundy County, August 2009

Betsy Stern, Cheatham County, August 2009

Hill Tract, Friends of Warner Parks, Davidson County, August 2009

State of Tennessee: TWRA, Davidson County, August 2009

Pat Sanders, Rutherford County, September 2009

Mark Skillman, Fentress County, September 2009

Linn Ann Welch, Cheatham County, September 2009

Kilpatrick Springs Farm LLC, Monroe County, December 2009

Steve and Susan Bass, Williamson County, December 2009

David and Sherry Pride, Williamson County, December 2009

Matt and Allison Mulliniks, Marshall County, December 2009

Diann and Lewis Walker, Cumberland County, December 2009

Ellen Jacobson and Grace Stewart, Davidson County, December 2009

Lynda Hughes Dawson, Greene County, December 2009

Wayne and Pamela Hughes, Greene County, December 2009

Chuck and Alice Belt, Grainger County, December 2009

James Williams, Sumner County, December 2009

Richard Kinzalow, Rhea County, December 2009

George and Ruby Dixson, Franklin County, December 2009

Jeff Jones, Warren County, December 2009

Lee Stapleton, Franklin County, December 2009

Estate of Juliette Mungovan, Davidson County, December 2009

Ronny Swafford, Bledsoe County, December 2009

H.J. Moser, Jefferson County, December 2009

John and Mona Lee, Williamson County, December 2009

Fred and Fay Baker, Hickman County, December 2009

Richard Hall, Hamilton County, December 2009

David Sapp and Jennifer Alvarez, Bledsoe County, December 2009

Finis and Gaynor St. John, Lincoln County, December 2009

David and Dwayne Laxton (Bear Creek Land Co.), Scott County,
 December 2009

Neal Family Farms LP, Maury County, December 2009

Theron Ris (Buck Branch Partnership), Dickson County, May 2010

Lee Hunter, Hickman County, June 2010

Friends of Radnor Lake, Davidson County, July 2010

The Estate of Sharon Sullivan, Williamson County, July 2010

Richard and Deloris Hammel, Lincoln County, August 2010

Kathleen Wolff and Jim Price, Davidson County, September 2010

Minda Lazarov and Barry Sulkin, Davidson County, September 2010

Richard West, Carroll County, September 2010

Rebecca and Joe Ingle, Davidson County, September 2010

Margaret Bernado, Davidson County, September 2010

George West, Davidson County, September 2010

Fiery Gizzard, The Conservation Fund, Marion County, November 2010

Bertha Fowler, Anderson County, November 2010

Miriam Gerber and Tom Smythe, Putnam County, November 2010

Pat Brumfield and Howard Harlan (Caney Fork Farms), Smith County,
 December 2010

Paul Putnam, Van Buren/White Counties, December 2010

Michael and Lindsay Wells, Williamson County, December 2010

Dave and Verlinda Waters, Meigs County, February 2011

Neil Martin, Hickman County, June 2011

Louise Manhein, Hardeman County, August 2011

Woodland Park Baptist Church, Hamilton County, August 2011

Pat Brumfield and Howard Harlan (Caney Fork Farms), Smith County,
 September 2011

Marge Ewers, Putnam County, October 2011

Battle of Nashville Preservation Society, Davidson County, October 2011

The Estate of Walter Wampler, Sullivan County, November 2011

John Barker and Don Mabry, Van Buren County, November 2011

Richard Simmers, Putnam County, November 2011

Dan Walling, Van Buren County, November 2011

Michelle Haynes, Sumner County, November 2011

Lucinda Trabue, Davidson County, December 2011

Gregory and Stephanie Sephel, Davidson, December 2011

Katherine Osten, Davidson County, December 2011

Maureen O'Hara Mowry, Davidson County, December 2011

Collins and Nancy Smith, Davidson County, December 2011

David and Lynn Barton, Davidson County, December 2011

Louis and Althea Jenkins, Davidson County, December 2011

Judy McCrary, Shelby County, December 2011

Bill and Lin Andrews, Marshall County, December 2011

Linda and Hal Moses, Davidson County, December 2011

Sharon and Elsie Bell, Bedford County, December 2011

Sam and Cyndie Swafford, Rhea County, December 2011

Geoff and Nancy Post, Marion County, December 2011

North Cove LLC, Marion County, December 2011

John, Carol, Joel, Michelle Kimmons; Patrick Ironwood, Sequatchie County,
   December 2011

Lynda Hughes Dawson, Hawkins County, December 2011

Mick Sullivan, Hickman and Dickson Counties, December 2011

Deanna Naddy, Maury County, December 2011

Rod and Kay Heller, Williamson County, December 2011

Pinnacle Point Partners, LLC, Hamilton County, December 2011

Hal Hardin, Wilson County, December 2011

Mary Ellen Stevens, Williamson County, July 2012

Acknowledgments

We extend our deepest appreciation to the many landowners whose farsighted decisions are helping to preserve Tennessee's green spaces. We are especially grateful to those of you who so graciously invited us into your homes and your personal stories. Thank you for your hospitality, your time, your openness, and your inspiration.

Our heartfelt thanks also goes out to the many people who helped make this book possible: To our editor, John, who guided us through this process with an abiding sense of calm and wisdom and fun. To Jeanie, for trusting us with this project and freeing us to let it unfold, and to the staff of The Land Trust for their assistance, especially Barbara, Emily, and Caitlin. To Bill, a graphic designer dream come true. To Ellen and the entire crew at Lithographics, especially Scott. To Caroline for tackling promotions. To Habib at Locomotion Creative, who helped us actualize our vision. And to the countless others who helped us along the way, including Jack Corn, Bill Allen, Barbara Logan, Caitlyn Gibbons, Laura Deleot, Todd Bottorff, and Don Matlock, as well as Rebecca Conard and her students at MTSU, Andra Kowalczyk and Jessica Davis, for their early work with The Land Trust oral histories, and Wayne Moore at TSLA for his work in the preservation of those transcripts. To our families, who made our jobs easier: Nick Rhoda (transcriber), "VV" Buntin (babysitter), Jeffrey Buntin, Sr. (consultant), and, of course, to Rich and Walker (ever-supportive husbands and biggest fans, whom we love). Thank you all.

Finally, we dedicate this book to Lucy McCall Knight, who passed on after she and her adoring husband, Dewey, shared their indelible story with us. Lucy, the land honors you with its buttercups, as do we with this book.

Nancy and Varina